A BACKPACKING GUIDE TO THE WEMINUCHE WILDERNESS

In the San Juan Mountains of Colorado

Dennis Gebhardt

The quote on page 153 is from <u>Zen and the Art of Motorcycle Maintenance</u> by Robert M. Pirsig, copyright 1974 by Robert M. Pirsig and published by William Morrow & Co., Inc.

Basin Reproduction and Printing Company
950 East Second Avenue
Durango, Colorado 81301
(303) 247-5212
First Edition April 1976
Second Edition January 1978
Third Edition January 1981
Fourth Edition January 1982
Fifth Edition February 1985
Printed in Durango, Colorado, United States of America

To Maria, who walked most of the trails with me
and spent long hours over my illegible manuscripts.

Drawings from the sketchbooks of Biff Stransky

Photographs by Dennis Gebhardt

ACKNOWLEDGEMENTS

Special thanks to Biff Stransky and Bill Humphrey for reading the manuscripts and subsequent words of advice. Also, thanks to the people of the San Juan and Rio Grande National Forest Supervisory and District Offices who have been helpful whenever possible.

PREFACE

The purpose of this guidebook is to provide information about the trails in the Weminuche Wilderness. The day is fast approaching when the Forest Service will begin limiting the number of people on certain trails. The fact is, most of the pressure is on 8 or 9 trails and the remaining 50 trails are used only infrequently. This distribution of hikers seems a little ridiculous, because many of the presently little-used trails have even more to offer in the way of a wilderness experience for backpackers. Only a very few are second-rate, and of course all such judgments are relative anyway; it is all wilderness. I delayed writing the guidebook for several years in the mistaken belief that a book of this kind would only attract more backpackers. Actually, the people will come and keep on coming in increasing numbers, guidebook or not. However, a guidebook could serve, in the process of providing up-to-date information about access and trails of the whole Wilderness, to make the backpacking public aware of the tremendous possibilities that exist in areas only lightly used at present.

No, the phenomenal growth of backpacking is not going to fade away just as suddenly as it began, with the packs and sleeping bags stored in attics for grandchildren to wonder over. The interest in backpacking is only a manifestation of the turning away from the seemingly single-minded worship and reverence assigned to the works of man. To be sure, fine things such as the arts and humanitarian works deserve the most exalted position possible, along with the prospect of lives made better by technology and medicine. The works of man that are woven into the essence of much of our civilization, such as the madness of the automobile, the desolate concrete canyons of cities, lives poured into jobs that cry out for humanism, and no space in which to draw a deep breath, are only a few of the reasons that so many people are in search of the works of Nature. Man in a great wilderness such as the Weminuche Wilderness must take Nature on its own terms and open his eyes to the beauty of the natural world. It seems that so much of modern man's life is "manufactured" in one sense or another, but wilderness is a refreshing reality.

Carl Jung said, "People who know nothing about nature are of course neurotic, for they are not adapted to reality." Unfortunately, there is darn little wilderness left with which to heal the neurotic masses. And the precious little that remains must not be despoiled. So for your part, preach a good wilderness ethic to those you encounter who seem in need of salvation; and when you are enjoying your next backpacking trip, if you notice a bit of trash some thoughtless person has left behind, carry it out yourself. Heavy use of this resource is intolerable because of the scarcity and irreplacable nature of wilderness. Personal efforts like this from all of us will preserve great natural treasures like the Weminuche Wilderness for the future.

TABLE OF CONTENTS

LOCATION 3

MAN'S HISTORY 5

GEOLOGICAL SUMMARY 9

FLORA AND FAUNA 13

MANNERS ON THE TRAIL 19

WEATHER, SAFETY, AND WILDERNESS TRAVEL 23

EQUIPMENT, CLOTHES, AND COOKING 33

USING THE NARROW GAUGE RAILROAD 41

TRAIL GUIDE 43

    I.   Needle Mountains Country 45

    II.   Vallecito Creek and the Pine River 67

    III.   The Volcanic Mountains 93

    IV.   South Fork of the Rio Grande Country 119

    V.   In the Bend 127

    VI.   Ute Creeks Country 141

    VII.   The Continental Divide Trail 153

SUGGESTED READING LIST 167

APPENDIX 169

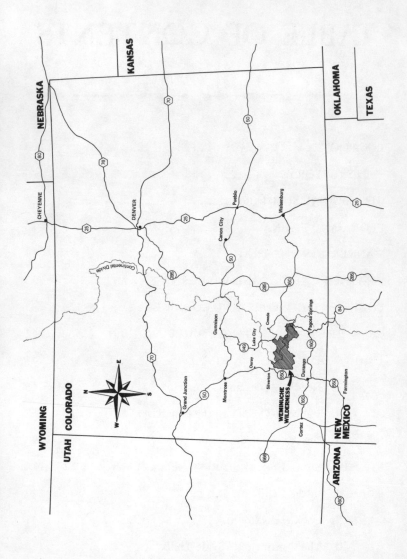

LOCATION

The Weminuche (Wem'-in-ooch) Wilderness was named after a smaller unit of the Ute Indian tribe of the same name who occupied the mountainous area which eventually became the Wilderness. To many people living in the immediate area, "Weminuche" refers only to the central section of the Wilderness surrounding Weminuche Creek on the San Juan side, Weminuche Creek on the Rio Grande side, and the headwaters of the Los Pinos River, Weminuche Pass. (Locally the name is frequently mispronounced with an extra syllable.) The extent of the expanded and recently designated Forest Service Wilderness is seemingly not comprehended by many persons. It is the largest wilderness area in Colorado (401,600 acres) as well as ranking very high in total acreage when compared to other wilderness areas in the forty-eight contiguous states.

The Weminuche Wilderness is located in the San Juan Mountains of southwestern Colorado with an eighty-mile stretch of Continental Divide as its backbone. The Continental Divide (which has a southerly trend through most of Colorado) has a westward bulge known as the "Bend", located about two-thirds of the way through the state. After Monarch Pass (U.S. Highway No. 50), at the south end of the Sawatch Range, the Divide begins angling southwest, and then from the La Garita Mountains, goes west. About 50 miles west, at Stony Pass and only a few miles from the town of Siverton, Colorado, the Continental Divide turns back eastward for about 80 miles to reach Wolf Creek Pass before resuming its southerly direction of travel. The Weminuche Wilderness is along and either side of the section of the Divide from Stony Pass to Wolf Creek Pass (on U.S. Highway No. 160), with the larger part to the south of the Divide. North, in the "Bend", are the headwaters of the Rio Grande. South of the Continental Divide, the rivers and creeks drain into the San Juan River, a major tributary of the Colorado River. The largest section of the Weminuche Wilderness that extends away from the Continental Divide at the south is the Needle Mountains and Pine River area at the western end of the Wilderness.

The Weminuche Wilderness is an area of great beauty and diversity. Most of the Weminuche is not as well-known as other wilderness areas in northern Colorado. Rough figures indicate that approximately 40% of the Weminuche Wilderness is barren rock, grass and water. The remaining 60% is forested lands. When compared to the large areas of rock and ice present in many of the nation's wilderness areas, the Weminuche Wilderness becomes a good representative of the diverse wilderness conditions of the western mountains before the occupation and parceling by man. Elevations within the Wilderness boundaries range from 7,910' to 14,083' and the average is over 10,000'.

MAN'S HISTORY

It is almost certain that the Anasazi, the prehistoric men who occupied the famous Mesa Verde ruins and other smaller sites in the San Juan basin, would have known of the existence and entered the section of the San Juan Mountains now known as the Weminuche Wilderness. Archaeologically, though, nothing found in the Wilderness confirms this. Little if any work has been done along this line.

Probably the first men to become intimate with the area were the Ute Indians. The Utes controlled most of the mountainous areas in the region of what is now Colorado and a sub-tribe, the Weminuche band, roamed over the area of the present day Wilderness in summer and wintered in the foothills to the south. The major trails in the Wilderness (e.g., Pine River Trail) were probably developed by the Weminuche Utes and information from the first white men to enter the area indicates this to be true. Even as late as 1900, the Utes still went to the upper Pine River and Vallecito country in the fall of the year to hunt deer and mountain sheep.

The first Europeans exploring in the area were Spaniards. Geographically, the barrier of the Continental Divide and Front Range of the Rockies was almost impenetrable. In addition, the settlements in eastern North America were initially unconcerned about the largely unknown area of the western mountains. This gave the Spanish a clear field for a long period of time. Santa Fe was in existence at the opening of the 17th century and the settlement of Abiquiu in 1778, only 100 miles distant from the Weminuche area, meant that the Spanish had plenty of opportunities for explorations northward. The big interest of the Spanish was in treasure and primarily in the gold that could be found in mountainous areas. The legends that exist and surround the Spanish presence in the area often include mention of the little known but alluring San Juan Mountains to the north. Since all subsurface rights belonged to the King of Spain, operations that removed valuable minerals would have been kept clandestine.

In 1776 the first recorded visit to the vicinity of the Weminuche Wilderness occurred when an expedition headed by two Franciscan priests, Escalante and Dominguez, went through the foothills to the south of the mountains with the goal of blazing a trail to connect Spanish settlements in New Mexico and California, and they named the San Juan, Piedra, Los Pinos, Florida, and Animas Rivers. In the 1820's a band of men called the Taos trappers, who ranged over much of the west seeking furs, undoubtedly penetrated the area and began bringing back information about the possibilities for exploitation. The Utes guarded the San Juans against the growing encroachments by mineral-seeking prospectors but as usual the overwhelming factor was the great numbers of white men who pushed aside the Indian. By 1860 an expedition of 200 men under Charles Baker entered the San Juans and explored mostly in the area of Silverton.

After the Civil War the westward expansion began in earnest and surveys were sent out to assess the largely unknown western lands. The Hayden survey of the 1870's probed the San Juans and the area of the Weminuche Wilderness with naturalists, geologists, surveyors, photographers and artists. Many of the highest peaks of the Wilderness Area were climbed and used for triangulation points (Mt. Eolus, Rio Grande Pyramid, Pagosa Peak, and South River Peak).

Although the main impetus for development was mineral exploration, the first huge herds of cattle (in 1876) and sheep (in 1882) soon entered the San Juan area. The bulk of the Wilderness was undoubtedly examined by prospectors and found to be unprofitable because of the small amounts of ore and hardships involved to remove it. For this reason it remained untouched. The exception is the area of the Needle Mountains and Piedra Pass but in comparison to the scale of the developments miners made north of Silverton, the effect was minimal.

Civilization of the San Juan Basin accelerated as the mining communities grew. The establishment of the National Forests was the first step in recognizing the value and extent of the mountainous lands in the San Juans. The San Juan National Forest was created in 1907 and the Rio Grande National Forest followed in 1908.

In the 20th century the main effect of man on the area of

the Wilderness was that of sheep and some cattle grazing. Logging and wide-scale water projects did not materialize for the same reason that the majority of the Wilderness was not extensively mined, that of extreme inaccessibility. Finally in 1932 the best sections of the Wilderness were set aside by the Forest Service as the Upper Rio Grande Primitive Area (56,600 acres) and the San Juan Primitive Area (240,000 acres). In 1971 a proposal for combining the old Rio Grande and San Juan Primitive Areas with additional expansion was made by the Forest Service. On January 4, 1975, the bill creating the 433,745-acre Weminuche Wilderness was signed into law.

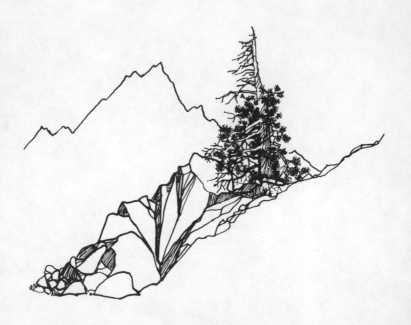

GEOLOGICAL SUMMARY

------- ◆ -------

The first mountains to appear where the present day San Juans are were of the Precambrian era about 600 million years ago. Precambrian rocks are the earliest records of geological processes. Rocks earlier than that have been so altered (or metamorphosed) that they are of little value in interpretations. The rock that represents these ancestral San Juans is a gneiss and schist complex that can be seen along the lower elevations of the Animas River canyon (the far western part of theWilderness) as a dark-colored and sometimes contorted layer.

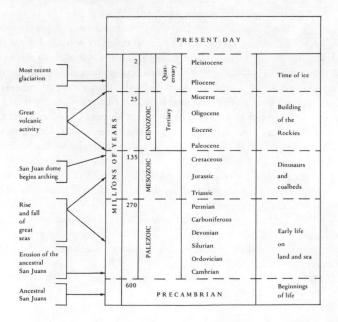

The Precambrian era was many, many times longer than all the rest of geologic time to present day, and there was ample time through the usual processes of erosion to reduce these early San Juans to a region of seas. The most significant event to take place before the end of the Precambrian era was some intense faulting and displacement amounting to what must have been tens of thousands of feet in the vicinity of what we now know as Elk Creek (in the northwest corner of the Wilderness). The Grenadier Range is the face of the fault block and this is represented today by many steep peaks just short of 14,000' in elevation. Some of the large scale folding caused by the displacements is easily seen when you descend to the Animas River via Molas Trail and again six or seven miles up Elk Creek Trail if you turn and face west and look at the mountains on the north side of the creek. Before the close of the Precambrian the gneiss and schist complex of the ancestral San Juans was intruded by a large amount of granitic rock which makes up the bulk of the high mountains in the western half of the Wilderness at present.

Geologic time through the Paleozoic era and up to the end of the Mesozoic era was marked by the area being dominated by the rise and fall of great seas. In the Cretaceous period, 135 million years ago, the stage was set for the structures of the present day San Juan Mountains to form. The Laramide Orogeny, which was a widespread geologic revolution bringing about the development of the great Rocky Mountain cordilleran chain, was being felt in the San Juan region by a great upwarping in the shape of a dome seventy to eighty miles to the east and west, and thirty to forty miles to the north and south over what is now southwest Colorado. As the Tertiary period came into existence the dome was arching upward to elevations of 10,000' or more. Erosion and glaciation began as soon as the dome gained relief above the surrounding country, and after a time it was reduced to 1,000' to 2,000' with the topography consisting of low, rounded hills and ridges (or monadocks) on a peneplain (Latin, pene — "almost").

The Tertiary period was a time of great volcanic activity, and deposits built up to depths of 10,000' of more. Actual relief was 3,000' to 4,000' because the massive overburden caused a downward settling.

At the beginning of the Quaternary period (the Pliocene epoch), about 12 million years ago, the topography was again reduced by the forces of erosion to a peneplain with monadnocks 200′ to 2,000′ high. The monadnocks were composed of the Precambrian rocks mentioned earlier and were preserved because of their hardness and resistance to weathering, as well as their remoteness from major stream drainages. Many of the high, flattened ridges (for instance, the Continental Divide between Elk Creek and Highland Mary Lakes) and many of the peaks that exist today in the Weminuche Wilderness are, in fact, those monadnocks.

Two more uplifts of the great dome took place with a volcanic interlude. Actually, the dome has had a history of more or less continuous uplift, punctuated by the massive, sustained uplifts referred to in the text. Approximately 2 million years ago the erosion and glaciation of the Pleistocene epoch began and in time, completely removed the volcanic accumulations from the western half of the Weminuche Wilderness. A north-south line placed a little east of the Granite Lake area divides the wilderness into the two different rock types: Precambrian granitic in the west and volcanic in the east.

The present day scenery in the Weminuche Wilderness is mostly a result of the Cerro, Durango, and most recently (10,000 years ago) the Wisconsin glacial periods. The U-shaped valleys, cirques, horn-shaped peaks, and other glacial features account for much of what is thought to be beautiful in the high, rugged mountain scenery.

FLORA AND FAUNA

MAMMALS

The Weminuche Wilderness is the home for many of the mammals commonly found in the western mountain states. Not long ago, the grizzly bear was the largest carnivore to inhabit the Wilderness. They could not tolerate the intrusion of man and sightings have not been confirmed for a number of years, although their existence in the remotest sections of the Wilderness is still a possibility, in my mind. The largest mammal in the Weminuche Wilderness is the elk. Once an animal of the plains, elk were introduced to western mountainous areas and have prospered. Elk spend their summers close to timberline in high basins and migrate away from the Wilderness to low country in order to avoid the harsh winter. Sightings of elk are common along the higher trails. Mule deer are present in large numbers, even more than elk, experts say, but are spread out over all elevations of the Wilderness. They do not band together like elk, and are more elusive when it comes to meeting man. Another large mammal is the black bear, which weighs up to 300 pounds. Black bears have blue, cinnamon, and black phases depending on the time of year and occupy the lower elevations of the Weminuche Wilderness. Bighorn sheep, the Colorado state animal, and mountain goats inhabit the crags and spires of summit areas. In 1964, the Colorado Game and Fish Department planted mountain goats near Lake City, Colorado, and these animals were soon observed in the Needle Mountains, an ideal habitat for them. Additional animals were then planted in Chicago Basin and appear to be doing well. Mountain lions exist in the wilderness and help keep the deer and elk population stable; but very little is actually known about the mountain lion population itself. All of the "big game" animals mentioned thus far are dependent on the existence of wilderness or near-wilderness conditions for their survival.

Coyotes, bobcats, badgers and weasels are a group of carnivores that efficiently control the numbers of smaller mammals. The coyote, much maligned by stockmen, is to be admired in the high mountains as it maintains hunting routes high amid peaks and ridges. The voice of the coyote, often echoing eerily off the rock walls, is the serenade of the western mountains.

Beavers and muskrats are found in streams. Lakes with beavers and their endeavors are most obvious to backpackers. Sometimes generations of beavers go into the construction and maintenance of a single còlony's site. The yellow-bellied marmot and pikas (rock rabbits) live in rocky places. The marmot's ease in traversing rockslides with a rippling of muscles as well as its piercing whistle are principal characteristics. Pikas have a "rubber-ducky" squeak and are observed making piles of hay in preparation for winter or jumping from rock to rock with mouths stuffed full of grass or wildflowers.

The western gray squirrel is found in forests at all elevations and the tassel-eared squirrel (also called the Abert squirrel) is in low elevations around Ponderosa pine. Chipmunks are of course present in quantity. Some other inhabitants of the forests are porcupines, skunks and snowshoe hares. Occasionally porcupines can be seen roaming above timberline as well.

Smaller mammals such as rock squirrel, golden-mantled ground squirrel, field mice, pocket gophers and shrews live in the Weminuche Wilderness. The obvious signs of pocket gophers are ridges or "ropes" of dirt seen just after the snow is melted. This small mammal, wishing to expand his tunnel network during winter, places the dirt removed from below in tunnels made in the snow.

BIRDS

At high altitudes there are a number of distinctive birds in the Weminuche Wilderness. The gray jay, with plaintive voice and friendly, sometimes beggar-like, attitude toward man, has earned the common name of "camp robber." Also close to timberline are the rosy finch, Clark's nutcracker, gray-headed junco, and the white-crowned sparrow. Above timberline is the habitat of the white-tailed ptarmigan, which is an expert of camouflage with its white in winter and mottled brown in summer. The golden eagle and, to a much lesser extent the bald eagle, can be seen soaring the skies above the Wilderness. The principal hawk is the red-tailed hawk. This husky bird avoids man in the mountains and claims a remote valley, hunts its meadows and gives a distinctive screech to intruders. The great-horned owl and the raven, two large birds, also have their homes in the Wilderness.

In cliff areas, the violet-green swallows in pursuit of insects or just enjoying the air currents are fun to observe. The blue and sharptailed grouse can be seen in the conifer forests along with downy and hairy woodpeckers.

In the meadows and along streams one will see the red-winged blackbird, the western bluebird and the western tanager, some beauties of the bird population. Seeking nectar from the scarlet gilia and other flowers are the hummingbirds. The many species of hummingbirds are difficult to distinguish with the exception of the broad-tailed hummingbird which is the only one to make the characteristic humming sound in flight. The rufous hummingbird is perhaps the most colorful. Hummingbirds are often seen when they fly close to a brightly-colored pack or item of clothing to give it an inspection for nectar.

Robins are found at practically all elevations and are companions of the backpacker who hears them singing a sleepy version of their usual song at dawn and dusk.

FISH

The waters of the Weminuche Wilderness have native trout (cutthroat), rainbow trout, brook trout and limited numbers of brown trout. The native trout were the only fish found in the cold higher waters of the West when man first arrived. In the Weminuche, the native trout occupy the high lakes and upper parts of stream drainages especially if the drainage has a major obstacle to the other species such as a large waterfall. Natives are not common to lower altitudes because they do not compete well with the rainbow and brook trout who can successfully occupy the same waters. Some very nice-sized fish have been taken from high elevation lakes in the Wilderness, particularly from 248' deep Emerald Lake, but on the average, because of the short growing season, the natives are frequently not over 12". Native trout spawn in spring through summer.

In certain lesser streams in the high country, small brook trout will be found in great numbers. Larger brook trout can be taken from the major drainages. Brook trout spawn from Septem-

ber to December. The rainbow trout favor the waters of the
Weminuche Wilderness and this popular fighting fish accounts for
much of the current angling successes. Rainbow spawn in the
spring in Colorado, the exact time dependent on altitude and water
temperature. Brown trout may be caught occasionally in the lower
elevations of the Wilderness and in the major creeks and rivers. A
hybrid, a cross of the native and rainbow trout, is sometimes
found in the waters of the Wilderness. In addition, a species of the
native, the Rio Grande cutthroat, may be found in the Wilderness'
tributaries of the Rio Grande.

Size of trout is normally regulated by the amount of water
present in the stream although many creeks in the Wilderness are
deceptive in appearance and possess some deep pools if a closer
look is taken. Run-off continues into July and fly-fishing opportunities are limited until later in the summer. The Colorado Fish
and Game Department has a program of aerial drops and they
stock many high altitude lakes in this manner. Naturally, a valid
Colorado State fishing license is required in the Weminuche Wilderness.

FLOWERS

The Weminuche Wilderness has dozens of species of wildflowers and it seems that if you visit the Wilderness every summer
you will find new ones. Flowers that are seen in the early summer
at lower elevations are often found in mid-summer as well in a
higher elevation. The snow melts and the earth warms in May and
June in the lower country but the alpine tundra is often melting
free in July and so the spring plants have a later start at that
elevation.

The first flower found after the snow is gone is the snowdrop,
a small white flower which blooms into the summer. At lower
elevations in boggy places, the yellow dogtooth violet (also known
as the glacier lily) is seen. After the earth has warmed sufficiently,
wild crocus, violets, wild lily-of-the-valley, bluebells and blue-
bonnets, holly-grape, buttercup, and spring beauty appear. If you
go into the mountains at different intervals in June you will see a
new array of flowers each time. Shortly after these spring flowers
have bloomed, the display begins in earnest: shooting stars or wild
columbine, showy and cutleaf daisies, larkspur, and cinquefoil.
Along wet places in June you'll often see the wild iris, a delicate

counterpart of its domesticated cousin. Dandelions are profuse at all elevations in the early season.

In mid-June and through July along the trail where it is dry and rocky, you can find the state flower of Colorado, blue columbine. Various shades of Indian paintbrush can be found now and throughout the summer at every elevation. Harebells, clematis (which from a distance resemble the columbine), fairyslipper (a rare orchid-type), chickweed, serviceberry and strawberry blossoms, thimbleberry, false lupine (also called yellow banner), scarlet gilia and yellow arnica are found in many kinds of forest cover and open meadow. Along the streams especially in meadows, you can find the tall, reddish-pink Parry's primrose, dark red roseroot, white marsh marigolds and numerous other flowers.

Along the highest parts of trails and on the Continental Divide, alpine flowers that are common are pink moss campion and white phlox, tiny flowers that find niches in the rocks for their home and which look like tiny jewels on the ground, yellow cinquefoil, paintbrush, and alpine sunflower.

In late summer you may see the purple mountain gentian. At certain times throughout the summer the rare red lily is found in protected and shady canyons. Many of these flowers are on the endangered list, so be careful not to pick or harm them.

TREES

The trees found in the Weminuche Wilderness are more easily identified according to their elevations than are the wildflowers. Trees found at lower elevations such as the narrowleaf cottonwood are not found higher, and likewise the subalpine fir, a high altitude species, usually does not grow below 10,000'. A southern sunny slope may encourage aspen growth perhaps as high as 11,000', but in general the trees found at certain elevations do not vary too much from their normal range.

At low elevations, up to 8,000' and possible even 8,500', deciduous trees such as narrowleaf cottonwood and boxelder can be identified. These trees prefer the banks of the streams and rivers in large open valleys. The foothills and trailheads at the Wilderness boundaries also support Ponderosa pine, Douglas fir and white fir. Some oakbrush is found in the same elevation as Ponderosa pine, and it provides a very colorful addition to the fall display.

In middle elevations approximately between 8,500' and

10,000', aspen becomes the deciduous tree. These beautiful tall white-trunked trees are called quaking aspen because of their shiny leaves, attached tenuously to the branches, which shimmer and shake at the slightest breeze. The golden to gold-red hues of the aspen in fall are a delight for the September wilderness traveler. Conifers at this level are the Englemann spruce, with their purple to reddish-brown bark. You will also see Colorado blue spruce, the state tree, which distinguishes itself from all other conifers in the Weminuche Wilderness with its blue-tinged needles which grow out in all directions from the twigs. A few white fir and Ponderosa pine can still be found at the lower reaches of this level, and extending down from the higher elevations are occasional subalpine fir. The aspen will be found on sunny southern slopes and open meadows; they become the "nurse" tree for the conifers after a burn. The northern slopes and darker canyons at the middle elevations will support the growth of spruces.

Between 10,500' and timberline, which is around 11,500' and 12,000' (higher timberline than common to the northern Rockies), the dark timber takes over in uniform and tight-packed stands. Subalpine fir is found in increasing numbers, and a variety of the subalpine fir, corkbark fir, is identified by its gray, rough, corky bark. Englemann spruce and Colorado blue spruce are also found at this level. On exposed slopes firs become twisted and contorted. At timberline and above, the cold temperatures and winds stunt the trees and cause them to grow close to the ground, resembling bushes. Trees at this elevation often freeze off above the normal snow depth, thus stopping the upward growth.

MANNERS
ON THE TRAIL

Unfortunately a good many people who enter the Wilderness seem to think that manners and courtesies are totally unnecessary. Maybe there was once a time when this was so. We now have sufficient numbers of people in wilderness areas to warrant consideration of others in their efforts to have a wilderness experience; it is equally necessary to exercise loving care when using the earth and walking among its creatures.

Probably one of the best resources of wilderness is solitude. Noisy people destroy wilderness serenity. You can disturb a neighbor who, unknown to you, may be camped only a couple of hundred yards away. Avoid noise in the form of radios and loud musical instruments as well as excessive shouting or screaming. Someone might even mistake your shouts for calls of distress and organize an unnecessary rescue attempt.

Your pets should be left home. If you must bring them, restrain them. Wild animals and bears in particular do not like domestic pets. Imagine your dog returning to camp with a couple of enraged cow elk at his heels! Besides causing trouble you would rather avoid, pets can annoy other hikers. No one appreciates rounding a corner only to meet a wildly barking dog, the owners of which are not in sight.

In regards to your impact on the land and its plant and animal populations, the often-quoted maxim, "take only pictures, leave only footprints," should summarize your code of behavior. One of the daily joys for me as a backpacker is leaving the place where I spent the night: where I had, relatively speaking, all necessities and comforts I required; they are now in the pack on my back and I can go without leaving a sign of my passing. Use of fire can leave a permanent mark on the wilderness. Aside from the obvious harm of letting fire rage uncontrolled into the forest, the controlled uses also leave scars. It is amazing how many people camping in a heavy use area, surrounded by the blackened stones of other fire rings, will gather more rocks and create yet another blackened circle. Before long, there isn't a decent looking stone of liftable size in sight. Small backpacking stoves such as Svea or Phoebus, a must above timberline at any rate, are better alternatives to the traditionalist's fire. Nevertheless, for many people a campfire is one of the most important features of outdoor living. To be sure, everyone should be skilled at firebuilding for emergency heat and survival situations. But there are many aspects of wilderness travel that can be better enjoyed without fire, ranging from the practical side (no more smudged cooking pots) to the aesthetic (letting your eyes adjust to the darkness and begin appreciating the other half of the daily circle, the nocturnal world).

If a fire is necessary and your campsite was previously untouched, erase all traces of the fire by scattering the stones and covering the ashes with forest duff to conceal the evidence. And of course, be sure all fires are out, dead-out and cold to the touch.

Concerning garbage, keep this in mind: you packed it in full, you can easily pack it out empty. A few people have the somewhat mistaken idea that the hills are filled with "rangers" whose business it is to follow the visitors and pick up all their leavings. I think this notion comes from National Parks where every employee seems to have the title "ranger". Let me assure you, the Forest Service budget for wilderness garbage detail is slim or nonexistent and if you leave something behind, it will probably stay there for a long time. When fishing, particularly in high altitude lakes, you should not throw fish entrails into the water, which will preserve them.

Please remember to dig a hole 6" to 8" deep for your bodily wastes and at the conclusion of the activity recover the hole with the sod you removed. Nature will take care of the decomposition very nicely if you do your part. If you make the hole deeper than 8" you will pass the layer in which biological decomposition is active. All other digging is to be avoided. You can usually find a spot for your tent that will drain rainfall naturally and require no ditching.

For washing and brushing your teeth, a small collapsible plastic or rubber washbasin can be carried so that these activities can take place well away from the sources of water. Use biodegradable soap.

Cutting live trees or foliage or collecting plant life is forbidden by the Forest Service except by special written permit. Resist the temptation to roll rocks. Don't cut corners on the trails where switchbacks are constructed since the erosion that follows will make your shortcut into an ugly scar. Observe all posted restrictions when entering heavy use areas.

MEETING HORSES

The two types of travel permitted in Forest Service designated Wilderness are foot and horseback. Almost anyone can take a backpacking trip. It is only a matter of adjusting the degree of difficulty to suit the condition of the participants. Horseback use enjoys quite a bit of popularity (especially in the Pine and Vallecito areas) and the person who uses the services of an outfitter does not have to face the wilderness completely on its own terms since quite a few amenities of life can be hauled along on the pack animals.

At times the two groups using the wilderness seem to be lacking in the ability to tolerate each other and this is unfortunate. The possibilities for co-existence are really much better between these two than if motorized use was introduced to wilderness trails. Walking through a mudhole churned by the hooves of a lengthy pack string is sure to arouse the ire of a backpacker whose first step into the morass is calf-deep; likewise in drier weather the choking cloud of dust that accompanies these enterprises is annoying. On the other hand, backpackers who think they should camp in the middle of the trail or the well-intentioned soul who crouches in hiding to assist the outfitter in passing but only succeeds in creating a mini-rodeo is not furthering his cause with the other side.

If you have not been around horses there are some characteristics that you should keep in mind. Horses are easily alarmed by things they don't understand or recognize, such as a person with a backpack. Swatting mosquitoes or other sudden movements can startle horses into kicking. When walking in dense cover you should call out a hearty hello to approaching horsemen. The sound of your voice lets the horse know you are a human being. Often you will meet riders who have little or no control over their animals. The horse can follow the animal ahead for miles with the rider holding the reins slack or not at all. Then when a dangerous situation arises, such as a grouse exploding into flight or the presence of cliffs, the rider is caught unaware. I always give horses the trail when in steep and rocky terrain and move off on the downhill side. If the horse begins to turn and buck the rider will have a better chance of bringing him back to the trail. Move off just far enough to avoid being kicked but not into concealment. Stand quietly but not absolutely still and, as said earlier, speak to the riders in a conversational tone of voice.

WEATHER, SAFETY, AND WILDERNESS TRAVEL

WEATHER FACTS

If you are planning a backpacking trip to the Weminuche Wilderness you have probably arranged your schedule months in advance. The possibility of bad weather would not change anything for most people; they would have to go on as planned. Some knowledge of what to expect from the weather could be of value. Decisions can then be made during your hike, decisions such as camping in canyons and valleys while a front is passing and then climbing up to the ridges and peaks in the clear, cool weather that follows, or deciding to take the trail on the high ridge earlier in the day and avoid the thunderstorm that will form later on.

To get an overall view of weather patterns it is good to read the weather maps published in the daily papers and watch the weather segment of television newscasts for at least a week prior to your trip. Some television stations give a few temperatures and only sketchy information about what is happening outside of their immediate area. Others do an excellent job of showing the location of storm fronts, their direction of travel, how intense the front may be, and other useful information such as satellite photographs and millibar charts. Try to get a general feeling for what will happen a few days to a week in advance.

The usual storm track for the San Juans is one that curves in a southeasterly direction from the northwest corner of the United States. Also large amounts of moisture can flow into the region from the south (Mexico and the Gulf of Mexico) and set off a lot of afternoon and evening showers, not needing a cold front to act as a trigger. The presence of a large high pressure system over southern Utah or the Four Corners area is a good indication of at least a few days of warm, dry weather. This high pressure system will sometimes modify the usual storm track so that the fronts moving in from the northwest will slide eastward along the border of Canada with no effect on the San Juan region.

Very specific information about the high mountain weather is not available (or reliable) because of the variability in the conditions present at high elevations. However, you can do your own forecasting of local weather with some degree of success. Local mountain weather is influenced by the presence of the mountains themselves. Air flow that is lifted upward in order to pass over a mountain range is cooled, and if enough moisture is present, there will be precipitation (orographic precipitation). The heating of the earth during the daytime and the cooling at night (diurnal variation) also tends to create local weather. Sometimes conditions create really violent thunderstorms with heavy rain, hail, or snow, severe lightning and high winds. These storms associated with no particular frontal system are very serious at times and can do damage and harm if you are in an unprotected place, even with the best of equipment.

Noticing changes in clouds and wind can form the basis for determining what the local weather in the San Juans will do. High, thin cirrus clouds (associated with the term "mare's tails") are often a sign of deteriorating weather and usually precede a frontal system by ten to twenty-four hours. A ring around the moon or sun caused by ice crystals in the stratosphere can be a pretty good indication that some sort of storm is on the way. The earlier in the day that a buildup of clouds begins, the more likely it is that a storm will result. Also, the higher the tops of the clouds grow, the more intense the storm will be.

Winds from the northeast, east or southeast are often moisture-bearing winds and this is a condition that assists in the development of a period of stormy weather. The westerly winds are usually dry winds and are present when fair weather is on hand. Winds that "back" from west to south to east (in a counterclockwise direction) are a good sign that the weather will deteriorate.

There are many phenomena that have a more obscure relationship to weather but can be helpful at times. A few of these are: sounds carry better in times of low pressure and high humidity; smoke rises straight up under high pressure (provided no wind is present) and follows the ground when the pressure is low; insects will be lower to the ground when the barometer is low and the swallows and other insect-catching birds that feed upon them will be flying correspondingly low.

WEATHER IN THE BACKPACKING SEASON (June, July, August and September)

JUNE: Because of its southerly longitude and a series of winters with limited precipitation, the Weminuche Wilderness generally went by the rule that the major trails would be snow-free by June 15th. June is just too variable, however, to make such generalized assumptions about conditions of the Wilderness trails. If you are in a position to know what kind of winter the San Juan Mountains have had, you will know more about what to expect in June. Mild winters have seen the higher trails open (although not in good shape) by early June. Following hard winters it has been difficult to get above 10,000' until the first week of July or later. High water is one of the major obstacles to travel in June. Streams are emptying the high country of snow and may be three or four times larger than normal.

On the positive side, June is usually a month of low precipitation and fair weather. Initially the nights are cold (close to freezing or below) but gradually they get warmer by July. The mosquitoes aren't out yet and the number of people is low. The first wildflowers appear and migratory animals such as the elk have begun moving up the valleys. The possibilities for June are enormous but it all hinges on the amount of the previous winter's snowfall.

JULY: Usually within a couple of days either side of the 4th of July, summer thunderstorms begin. The rising temperature of the earth and the presence of moisture-bearing winds cause these local disturbances which usually pass in an hour or two. Extended rainy periods indicate the presence of a front. The mosquitoes will have come out in full force in July and the streams begin to clear up and drop to a more normal level. This is the warmest month and temperatures may be as high as the 80's occasionally; at night, 40's and high 30's. The moderate temperatures are favored by most people, and from the 4th of July on the vacationers have come to the Weminuche. Wildflowers are also at their best during July. By the end of July or beginning of August stream and lake temperatures have reached their maximums.

AUGUST: From about the middle of August the daily temperatures begin dropping and a chill, foretelling the approaching fall, is often in the air. The weather is very unpredictable in August.   There may be a succession of weeks of fair and mild, beautiful weather, or it may be one of the rainiest months of the whole summer.

SEPTEMBER: This may be the best month for the Weminuche. It is, on the average, a month of low precipitation although some of the worst floods on record came around Labor Day. The temperatures drop to freezing almost every night and storms may possibly bring snow as well as rain but it will melt away the next day. The streams are now at their lowest point and some of the small impermanent ones will dry up. Sometime in September the first golden colors appear in small patches in the aspen high up on the mountainsides and begin spreading downward. The unique whistle of the bull elk can be heard echoing through the forest. The places that were heavily used during summer will be deserted and you will have the Weminuche to yourself.

LIGHTNING

Lightning can be a real concern for the backpacker in high mountains such as the San Juans. It can be erratic and illogical and you are never completely safe, but most of the time it strikes in fairly predictable ways. Lightning prefers to strike the highest point or peak, the edge of cliffs, a large isolated tree, or the largest object in meadows or open flat areas. Rarely does a storm with lightning appear over you without warning. You can gauge approximately how far away the storm is by allowing five seconds for each mile between the time when you see the strike and hear the thunder. If you are caught in a bad position with no hope of retreat authorities recommend that you crouch down (not lie down) on some kind of dry insulation such as sleeping pads or ropes. Also you should divest yourself of all metal objects since their presence could cause serious burns if a strike does occur. Stay at least 50′–80′ from cliff faces because of the possibility of charges radiating from the edges. Small shallow caves must also be avoided. In the event that someone is struck by lightning, immediately begin heart massage and mouth-to-mouth resuscitation.

HEAT, COLD, AND ALTITUDE

The wilderness traveler should be aware of the problems created by excesses of heat, cold, and high altitude. Books have been written about these subjects, but more than a brief discussion is beyond the scope of this guidebook.

The less a person engages in strenuous exercise in his daily life, the less likely his circulatory system is able to cope with extremes of heat and cold. Although the highest temperatures in the mountains rarely exceed the 70's or 80's, heat exhaustion and heat stroke are possiblities. Heat exhaustion, attended by weakness, dizziness, cramps, and rapid pulse, should be treated by getting the victim out of direct sunlight, resting, drinking fluids, and taking salt tablets. Heat stroke, accompanied by the preceding symptoms in addition to loss of consciousness, should also be treated by cold water baths to lower the body temperature and immediate professional help should be sought since it can be fatal.

Assist your body in regulating its temperature by adding and subtracting items of clothing to compensate for external changes due to time of day and altitude. When exertion causes sweating, be sure to replace your fluid loss by drinking plenty of water and taking salt tablets. Losses of water at high altitudes could amount to as much as three to four quarts a day without exertion. Caution should be used in exposing your skin to the sun, and when you spend extended periods above timberline a sun-blocking product such as glacier cream will be required for your face. Sunglasses provide valuable protection for your eyes from the more intense radiation received from the sun at high altitudes.

Combinations of rain, sleet, snow, wind, and exhaustion can lead to a condition known as hypothermia even in summer. It has been stated that hypothermia is the most common cause of wilderness deaths. Hypothermia is a condition in which the victim's body temperature drops too low to sustain life. Symptoms are: shivering and becoming chilled even with exercise and a confused and eventually apathetic state of mind. To treat a victim of hypothermia, wrap in dry, warm clothing and administer hot fluids. Sometimes the only way to warm the victim is to transfer body heat from a warm person, best accomplished by getting into a sleeping bag together.

In some instances people from altitudes close to sea level are susceptible to a sort of illness brought on by the thinner air above 8,000'. This mountain sickness has symptoms such as headache, a feeling of weakness, poor appetite, dizziness, impaired judgment, and is accompanied by pulmonary edema in severe cases. Sufficient time should be spent in acclimating yourself, a process in which the blood increases its proportion of oxygen-carrying red blood cells, rather than racing to the highest elevations on the first day.

FIRST AID KIT

For even the shortest wilderness excursions some sort of first aid kit is necessary. You can buy commercially prepared kits that are light in weight and admirably suited to backpackers' needs for around five dollars. You can also assemble the necessary items from a drugstore and your home medicine chest. The advantage of assembling your own is that you can add items as your need for them becomes apparent. List 1 consists of the basics, most of which you are likely to have on hand around home. List 2 represents items that you will want to add to list 1 as your trips become multi-day affairs and your wilderness destinations become more remote. For longer trips and/or more people quantities will have to be increased, and you will probably want to add items like inflatable splints and antibiotics as the trip begins to take on the aspect of an expedition.

LIST 1	LIST 2
Antacid tablets	Ace elastic bandage
Bandaids (assorted sizes)	Adhesive tape (roll)
Chapstick	Butterfly closures
Manicure scissors	Darvon (prescription pain reliever)
Moleskin	Dramamine
Mosquito repellant	Gauze (roll)
Safety pins	Glacier creme
Salt tablets	Lomotil (prescription antidiarrheal)
Sun glasses	Merthiolate
Sun lotion	Razor blade
	Tweezers
	Vaseline (small tube)

WILDERNESS TRAVEL

Among hikers, veteran and tenderfoot alike, there is probably no more widespread ailment than the blister. A combination of light and heavy socks and a pair of shoes that have been broken in usually minimize this problem. The best medicine for blisters is preventive; that is, when you first feel a warm or irritated spot on your foot, stop and apply a piece of moleskin cut to fit the area. The moleskin patches can be left on until the trip is over. As a last resort, well-formed blisters with water under the skin may be treated by puncturing with a sterilized needle. Keeping broken or opened blisters clean is of the utmost importance since infection could be a very serious complication.

Ticks are frequent in the first half of summer and transfer to your clothes from brush and foliage through which you may pass. Most ticks are found before they have entered the skin since they seem to roam around for a few hours looking for the best site. Treatment of your clothes and especially your trousers with insect repellant is helpful in tick season. In the event that a tick has penetrated the skin there is the possibility of tick fever although the chances of getting tick fever from an encounter are really quite low. A tick can usually be induced to back out of the skin by bringing the flame of a match or perhaps a swab soaked in fuel close to its head. When extracting a tick be sure you get the head along with the body. Frequent inspections of yourself throughout the day are the best line of defense.

No rattlesnakes are found in the area since the lowest elevations of the Wilderness are above those occupied by rattlesnakes.

Water in the Weminuche Wilderness, as a general rule, is pure and safe for drinking with the following exceptions: when you suspect the activities of persons upstream of you, water flowing from old mines, or water from stagnant pools.

Where the animals that exist in the Wilderness are concerned, enjoy them from a distance and avoid any confrontations either knowingly or unknowingly. Animal mothers from the smallest to the largest are ferocious in attacking if you appear to be a threat to their young. They have absolutely no way of knowing that you intend no harm by your approach. Be careful of circumstances that might accidently lead to the cornering of a wild animal. Most animals will give our species a wide berth if at all possible. No firearms are necessary, either.

Put your food in airtight plastic bags and keep a clean camp at all times. The wilderness bear population is not accustomed to foraging for garbage but a messy camp with overpowering smells of food could encourage them.

When getting ready for bed there are certain items that you should not leave unprotected when you are sleeping. Porcupines and other small mammals have been known to eat cotton and wool clothing, leather (shoes) and canvas for salt or natural fiber. If

items are left in a tightly closed nylon pack they should be safe
for the night.

Before entering the Wilderness make sure someone is in-
formed of your plans (and check in with them on your return),
your car is parked in a safe place and does not impede other
vehicles at the trailhead, and your keys, change, tickets, etc., are
safely put away. Sign all trail registers.

FORDING STREAMS

Traveling the trail system of the Weminuche Wilderness
involves many stream crossings. Usually until mid-summer when
the run-off has ended, many of these crossings are difficult and
perhaps impossible (e.g., the Animas River). Normally it will be
okay to take off your shoes, socks and trousers, and wade bare-
footed. If there isn't sufficient room for your shoes in the pack,
you can tie the shoelaces together and hang the shoes around your
neck. A stick is always helpful in balancing as you cross the larger
streams or rivers. It may be necessary to wear your shoes in order
to protect your feet if you are crossing a wide, cold stream with
possible sharp rocks or big boulders. Loosen your waist belt so
that you can throw your pack off if you lose your balance and fall
into the water. On reaching the other side, put on dry socks and
empty the water from your shoes. Well-waterproofed shoes will
dry quickly.

ROUTE – FINDING

Although the unmaintained and difficult-to-follow trails
are indicated on the guidebook maps as manways, even some of the
better trails can have sections where the way does not seem clear.
This is particularly common in meadows or clearings where traffic
tends to spread out, leaving no discernible path to follow. In
addition, an active stream can obliterate the trail for a number of
yards on either side. The Forest Service puts their "i" blaze on
trees along the trails and erects rock cairns and post-markers to
assist the traveler. Careful examination of the trees at the opposite
side of a meadow or stream will usually reveal a blazed tree and the
trail. The U.S.G.S. topographic maps have the vegetated and
forested areas indicated with green to distinguish them from
clearings. Do not confuse this with Forest Service maps where
green indicates National Forest property and white, private prop-

Small and large rock cairns

Post-marker   Blazed tree

erty. The approximate relationship of the trail to meadows and
other topographic features can be valuable information to the
backpacker.

GETTING LOST

Having good maps of the area and practicing and constantly
improving your map-reading skills are some ways to help you gain
knowledge about unfamiliar country. The excellent U.S.G.S. series
of 7½' and 15' quadrangles are available from local shops or can be
ordered from a U.S.G.S. office (see appendix). You should observe
landmarks and make mental notes as you approach them as well as
when they fall behind you. If you realize you are lost, immediately sit down and think. Wildly trying to retrace your steps may
only make your situation worse. Sit, think, study your maps and
surroundings, and listen for sounds that may give you clues. Fear
and panic are usually not far below the conscious level of the mind
and will invade your thoughts very quickly unless you exercise
some self-discipline.

There are many techniques for telling time, for finding
direction, and for surviving a wilderness emergency. It is wise to
mark your route as you try to find your way to known country.
This may assist a search party in following you and you will know
you have been traveling in a circle if you stumble onto your own
markers. The sun and moon rise and set roughly from the east to
the west. Head for streams and valleys because in the Weminuche
Wilderness the major drainages will eventually lead to civilization.
And so on. There are many books and much information in the
field of survival. Learn as much as you can of the various techniques of survival for you never know when they may be useful to
you.

EQUIPMENT,
CLOTHES,
AND COOKING

In keeping with the scope of this guidebook, I am hoping to emphasize the kinds of equipment and clothes that would be especially pertinent to the summer visitor of the high Southern Rocky Mountains and in particular the Weminuche Wilderness. People who are used to other mountain ranges with different elevations, seasons and longitudes will have worked out the problems of heat, cold and wet in a manner suitable to their locality. The equipment listed here is what I and other people have found to be suitable for the San Juan Mountains.

EQUIPMENT

Sleeping bag: Temperatures in June through September can easily fall to the teens. A sleeping bag which you feel will sleep comfortably down to 10 or 15 degrees will probably be adequate for the high mountains. Currently the most popular bag type is the bag with goose or duck down filler, constructed in a mummy or semi-mummy shape and internally baffled for light-weight warmth. There are some very nice bags with Fiberfill II and Polarguard filler coming on the market for $60 to $80. Avoid the low-priced and probably poorly-constructed ones. The advantage of bags with man-made filler is that they do not lose loft when wet. The clear disadvantage is the weight, in some cases two pounds more than a down bag of comparable warmth. The name of a reputable sleeping bag manufacturer means a great deal, since you really have no way of knowing about the internal quality of construction and filling material. If you plan to use a tent most of the time, you can count on temperatures being 5 to 10 degrees higher which means you will not need as warm a bag. Lay your sleeping bag out in the air and sunshine each morning for an hour or two to freshen it and rid it of moisture accumulated during the night. This is especially important with down bags if you wish to maintain their loft. Money spent on quality equipment is a good investment and one you won't regret when the temperature drops. A pad of ensolite or foam beneath your bag is light-weight to carry and will make a lot of difference in sleeping comfort and warmth.

Backpack: The frame of a good backpack should be made of aluminum alloy, contoured to your body and equipped with well-padded and adjustable shoulder and waist straps. Pay particular attention to the quality of the waist belt since this is where the effort of carrying is concentrated. You should probably avoid purchasing packs with packbags that are the large undivided expedition type. You will be tempted to stow away unnecessary items and unless you are pretty experienced in loading backpacks and used to heavy loads, the large backpack could be too much of a good thing.

To get your pack to ride correctly, slip it on and keep the shoulder and waist straps relatively loose; then take a deep breath and shrug your shoulders as high as you can and tighten the waist belt. When you relax you can make the shoulder straps snug (not tight) and the load will be about 90% on your hips. Evenutally you won't have to change the shoulder strap adjustment when you take off or put on the pack.

Tarps and tents: Tarps made of nylon or plastic can be rigged in ingenious ways to form shelters for the backpacker. As well as being inexpensive, these shelters are lightweight and practical for use in the milder weather below timberline. Above timberline where you will be exposed to the full force of storms, something more in the way of a shelter is required. Although some new designs incorporating the shape of the dome look promising, the tried and tested A-frame high altitude tent with a rainfly is your best bet at present. There are usually tents for sale in the $20 to $50 range that are a waste of money. You would be better off with the tarp and its simplicity. Plan on paying $90 for the low and $125 on the average for a quality high altitude tent. And with that good a tent you will want to use a ground sheet to protect the floor. Practice pitching your tent before you make a trip with it. If a black cloud is rapidly blotting out the horizon, you won't want to waste any time in setting up your tent.

CLOTHES

Shoes: Children and youths might do all right with some kind of sneakers, preferably ankle high; but what has proven best is a leather lace-up hiking boot. A shoe with padding on the inside and Vibram soles is almost a necessity for rugged mountain terrain. Your shoes should be a comfortable fit with two pairs of socks, light and heavy. The larger the load you are carrying and the rougher the terrain on which you expect to walk, the more substantial your boots must be. For psychological reasons you may feel better with a lighter boot but don't let this override the fact that you need a sturdy shoe with good support for safe wilderness travel. Most of the better shoes are imports and consequently carry a pretty high price tag. So far there are only a few American companies interested in producing a quality backpacking shoe. Waterproof your boots after each trip with the product recommended by the retailer or manufacturer.

Socks: The combination that proves best for most people is a light cotton or nylon inner sock and a heavy wool (ragg) outer sock. Take an extra set so you have something to change into since there are many stream crossings in the Wilderness trail system.

Trousers: Trousers made of cotton (levis, for example) are adequate in almost all situations. It is probable that most of the miles covered on wilderness trails have been walked by people wearing some sort of sturdy cotton jeans. High quality wool trousers are also excellent because when wet, wool will still keep you warm. Shorts can be worn with some success depending on the time of year and how fierce the mosquitoes are.

Shirts: Long-sleeved shirts are convenient because you have the option of rolling up the sleeves for cooling, or using the full sleeve length when you need warmth. Wool shirts might be a little too warm for extensive hiking in mid-summer. Long-sleeved cotton work shirts are practical and inexpensive. Fish-net undershirts are highly recommended since they can heat or cool your body depending on how you ventilate at your shirt front.

Sweaters and parkas: A plain wool pullover sweater is the choice of many backpackers but if you are one who is often cold you may want a down vest or parka. As with the sleeping bags, down is warmer per pound but next to useless if soaked with water.

Rain gear: For wet weather your choice is between a raincoat with rain pants or chaps, and an all-covering poncho. You can buy products made of cheap plastic but the durability will be minimal. You get pretty much what you pay for and good quality rain gear is around $45 for a complete outfit or $30 for a poncho, which is also useable as a shelter.

Hat and mittens: Some kind of hat is desirable for protection from the sun, and in cooler weather a stocking cap does a fine job of conserving your body's warmth. Mittens or warm gloves will be appreciated in the morning and evening during a cold spell.

Your rain parka combined with a sweater over a shirt and undershirt will usually provide the warmth necessary for summer in the high mountains. There is often a short period after you get out of your sleeping bag when you wish you had an expedition parka, but you must be willing to persevere for a few minutes while you wait for the pokey sun to climb high enough to shine into your camp.

COOKING

Cooking equipment doesn't need to be elaborate to be effective. For serving you can use two plastic cups or Sierra cups and spoons. You could make do with one cup and spoon but I prefer to have a hot drink to go along with the food. One or two people can get along fine with a one quart pot. A tight fitting lid for the cooking pot conserves appreciable amounts of fuel. Manufacturers of freeze-dried foods say you don't need to cook their dinners; to eat, simply pour hot water into the package and wait a few minutes. It can be done this way but it tastes better if you cook the meal for a few minutes to really make it palatable. If you have time, letting the dinner soak in its water an hour or two before heating reconstitutes the meal more completely and improves the flavor.

Stoves: In "Manners on the Trail", I advocated the use of backpack stoves by wilderness travelers. In addition to the reasons given in that section, I must point out that fine control of heat, ease of lighting in all conditions, and availability of more free time (since there is no need to gather firewood) are also among the advantages of a lightweight stove. Their only disadvantage is the weight of slightly more than a pound in addition to small amount of fuel necessary for each day of operation. Using these stoves for cooking and wearing adequate clothes for warmth have completely eliminated the need for fire. In the over 800 miles of hiking during the past two years, I have never built a fire and my conscience is soothed to know that my mark on the wilderness is minimal. Follow the directions that come with the stove and once you are acquainted with its operation you will find it to be an outstanding performer. Some hints for operating your stove are: don't use leaded gas; don't fill the tank more than two-thirds full since overfilling could result in overheating; don't let it run until the fuel supply in the tank is exhausted, because it will scorch the wick resulting in poor operation. Shelter your stove from wind while cooking to improve its efficiency. You can use a plastic eye dropper to put fuel into the priming cup. White gas is very flammable so be extremely careful when the fuel bottle is open!

Food: There is a wide variety of freeze-dried food now available to backpackers. You have to decide under what circumstances its convenience and light weight override the higher cost. A lot of people buy the freeze-dried main dish one-pot-meals from backpacking shops and get the rest of the food from grocery stores. Items such as powdered drinks, crackers, cheese, dried fruit, dried soups, biscuit mixes and granola can round out the menu. Pemmican and jerky, standbys of the mountain men, can be made at home. Check to see what ingredients need to be added to your grocery store foods since you may not be able to use some of them on the trail if they require a lot of preparation. As you gain altitude you will increase cooking time, and anything that takes more than half an hour to cook will use too much fuel. Grocery store foods are generally too heavy because of the fact that they are often packaged in cans or jars and include some liquid. Repacking food from the supermarket is an alternative to carrying a heavy can or un-resealable plastic wrapper. Neverthless, some canned items will still be impossible to take. The foods that lend themselves well to repackaging are the ones that are dry-packed, such as nuts, raisins or dried meat. These can be placed in a zip-lock bag or one that can be reclosed with a twist-tie. The plastic storage bags used for re-packaging can be recycled as garbage bags. For long trips, plan two or three days' rations and package them together so you don't need to remove all your food from the pack each time you prepare a meal.

There are many excellent books that go into great detail on all phases of equipment, clothes and cooking. Catalogs can also be informative to study. Equipment could easily become a fetish though, and when buying new equipment ask yourself, "Is it really vital to my health, safety or enjoyment of the wilderness?" Obviously, a single purpose item such as a sleeping bag is; pocket altimeters or unnecessary items of clothing may not be. Sadly, more than a few people think that equipment is the whole point of backpacking. Equipment is only a tool, a freedom-giving tool that lets you penetrate the natural world around you.

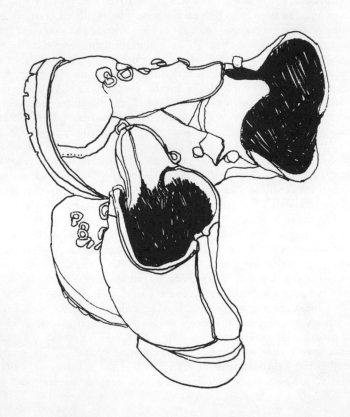

THIS LIST IS TO HELP YOU ORGANIZE AND SELECT YOUR EQUIPMENT FOR A BACKPACKING TRIP.

COOKING
backpacking stove w/funnel for filling
fuel bottle with extra fuel
plastic eye dropper
matches
saucepans with lids
spoon
pocket knife
cups, plastic or Sierra
plastic canteen or water bottle
G.I. can opener
miscellaneous containers
plastic garbage bags
biodegradable soap

FOOD IDEAS
granola or instant hot cereal
instant coffee
instant hot chocolate drink
instant orange juice
powdered milk, made richer by
    adding Coffee-mate
freeze dried foods
dried soups
raisins
cheese in a squeeze tube
crackers
jerky or dried meat
flour or corn tortillas
peanut butter
teabags and sugar
powdered fruit drink
nuts
tropical chocolate (won't melt)
space food sticks
hard candy
salt and pepper
dried herbs and seasonings

SHELTER / SLEEPING
ground sheet
tarp or mountain tent
1/8" nylon cord
steel skewer stakes
sleeping bag and stuff sack
ensolite or foam pad
tie-on straps

CLOTHING AND PACK
backpack and frame
boots
socks, light and heavy pair
extra socks
camp shoes
long johns or fishnet
long pants
shorts
long-sleeved shirt
wool sweater
poncho or raincoat
rain chaps
hat
mittens or gloves
bandanas
down jacket or vest

SURVIVAL
candle or hexamine tablets
first-aid kit
flashlight and extra battery
extra food
extra sweater
maps and compass
waterproof matches
fishline and hooks

MISCELLANEOUS
toilet paper
plastic trowel
needle and thread
ripstop repair tape
spare pack parts
camera and film
lightweight binoculars
rubber bands
plastic washbasin
watch
toothbrush and toothpaste
comb
small mirror
notebook and pencil
extra nylon cord

USING THE
NARROW GAUGE
RAILROAD

The tracks of the Narrow Gauge Railroad first reached Silverton from Durango in 1882 and this was considered quite an engineering feat. The tracks were even extended to Red Mountain Pass and up the Animas River and Cement Creek north of Silverton in a few years. As mining activity tapered off, freight and passenger service to Silverton were the main purposes for the railroad's existence after the twentieth century began. The same engines and coaches are still operating today and two trains make the daily trips to Silverton from Memorial Day through the end of September. Although this is still a legitimate railroad the business is tourist-oriented and vacationers, train buffs and photographers in particular, amount to 1,000 people a day, riding the train from Durango to Silverton and back. Over the years the train made flag stops in the Animas canyon for prospectors and their supplies. Climbing parties interested in the Needle Mountains and some fishermen began using the railroad in this manner also. Then over the last 10 or 15 years when the number of people who wanted to go backpacking mushroomed, the train began hauling as many as 2,000 backpackers a summer to Needleton and Elk Park.

The Narrow Gauge Railroad sells round trip and one-way tickets to Needleton and Elk Park. Anyone who wishes a one-way ticket from Needleton or Elk Park to Durango must have the cash ready for the conductor when boarding the train (no personal checks). The D. & R. G. W can issue tickets for particular days if so desired. So far, this has not been done but the management indicates that the number of backpackers is becoming exasperating. Reservations should be made in advance. When flagging down the train, the prescribed method is to stand on the engineer's side of the tracks (right side in the direction of travel) and wave a white cloth horizontally in front of you. No dogs are allowed to board the train. Backpacks are stored behind the rear seats of the cars.

The railroad frowns on walking along the tracks in the

canyon and it is a dangerous practice. With the Animas River roaring by the tracks, it is possible that the approach of a train would not be heard. In addition, there are narrow places which would not allow room for you and the train both. The tracks are the D. & R. G. W.'s private property. There is no trail along the east side of the Animas River between Needleton and Elk Park. There are no services at either of these stops, only accesses to Columbine Pass Trail (No. 6) at Needleton, and Elk Creek Trail (No. 4) at Elk Park. The address and phone number of the D. & R. G. W. depot in Durango are found in the appendix of the guidebook.

TRAIL
GUIDE

The trails are numbered No. 1 through No. 59 in the guide-book. The numbering system begins at the northwest corner with No. 1 and continues through the San Juan National Forest side to Wolf Creek Pass, stopping at No. 39. On the Rio Grande Side, the numbers begin at Wolf Creek Pass with No. 40 and proceed into the Bend to reach No. 58. The Continental Divide Trail, No. 59, stretches across the entire Wilderness.

The trailheads (where the road ends and the trail begins) are referred to by their geographic name and a code letter; for example: Purgatory Campground, trailhead (D). If a trail does not have a trailhead letter this means that it begins on another trail at a certain point which is fully explained in the trail description.

The Forest Service has a system of gravel roads on which almost all of the trailheads are found. The road system is numbered on the free-issue visitors maps and these road numbers (e.g., No. 631) are included in the guidebook directions to a particular trailhead.

The guidebook maps represent the most up-to-date information on the Wilderness trail system. The author walked the trails and corrected discrepancies in the U.S.G.S. 7½' and 15' quadrangles, and the data has been incorporated into the guidebook maps. Pertinent landmarks (ridges and peaks) and their elevations are shown, as well as streams and lakes. Use of the U.S.G.S. quadrangles is recommended in addition to the maps with the guidebook. You should study and compare the information available from both. Don't wait until you are on some trail and hopelessly confused.

The Forest Service free-issue visitors' maps have been recently updated and provide trail information useful in a more general way. By this I mean the Forest Service map is generally correct where the trail's relationship to topographic features is concerned but, because of the small scale of the map, will represent a large number switchbacks with only one or two and does not detail small deviations from the route. A special Weminuche Wilderness trail map will be produced shortly by the Forest Service.

The Rio Grande National Forest map displays the assigned numbers of their trails (No. 810, No. 811, etc.) and these are noted in the trail descriptions for that section of the Wilderness.

The guidebook readers are encouraged to make use of the vertical ascent and descent in arriving at realistic trail mileages. For instance, East Ute Creek Trail (No. 55) has 1,363' of vertical ascent in 3.5 miles. 1,363' divided by 5,280' (1.0 mile) yields about .25 mile which should be figured into the total 3.5 miles of East Ute Creek's Trail, making 3.75 miles a more accurate figure for the length of the trail. Or, Endlich Mesa Trail (No. 9), has 3,243' of vertical ascent and 1,803' of vertical descent for a total of 5,046' elevation difference enroute. This amounts to nearly another 1.0 mile to be added to the stated length.

I.
Needle Mountains Country

—————•◆•—————

	trailhead	length
No. 1 — Cunningham Gulch Trail	(A)	.2.5 miles
No. 2 — Highland Mary Lakes Trail	(A)	.3.0 miles
No. 3 — Molas Trail	(C)	.4.0 miles
No. 4 — Elk Creek Trail		.9.0 miles
No. 5 — Purgatory Creek Trail	(D)	.11.0 miles
No. 6 — Columbine Pass Trail		14.25 miles
No. 7 — City Reservoir Trail	(E)	.12.7 miles
No. 8 — Florida Trail	(F)	.6.0 miles
No. 9 — Endlich Mesa Trail	(G)	.13.0 miles

75.45 miles

The Needle Mountains country is a tight-packed mass of high peaks and scenic beauty at the western end of the Wilderness. The three 14'ers, Eolus, Windom and Sunlight are located here as well as many others which reach nearly as high and large numbers of summits named and unnamed over 13,000'. The trails at the northwest corner are at the edge of the fabulous Silverton mining district and there are occasional mineral prospects throughout the Wilderness in section I. Trails No. 1, No. 2, and No. 4 ascend to the Continental Divide before it swings east to miss the Needle Mountains. The Narrow Gauge Railroad passes the western border of the Wilderness through the Animas River canyon and makes flag stops for trails No. 4 and No. 6. This in addition to the attention focused on the Needle Mountains by climbers, makes these trails fall into the category of heavy use. Trails No. 3 and No. 5, although not in the Wilderness, pass through wilderness-type country and are very important accesses to the Needle Mountains area. No. 8, also not in the Wilderness, is presented as an alternative to the difficult access on No. 7.

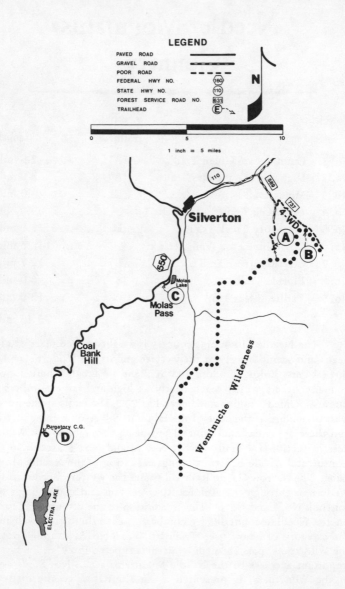

LEGEND

PAVED ROAD	
GRAVEL ROAD	
POOR ROAD	
FEDERAL HWY NO.	160
STATE HWY NO.	110
FOREST SERVICE ROAD NO.	631
TRAILHEAD	E

N

0   5   10

1 inch = 5 miles

110

689

737

Silverton

4-WD

A

B

550

Molas
Lake

C

Molas
Pass

Coal
Bank
Hill

Purgatory C.G.

D

Weminuche Wilderness

ELECTRA LAKE

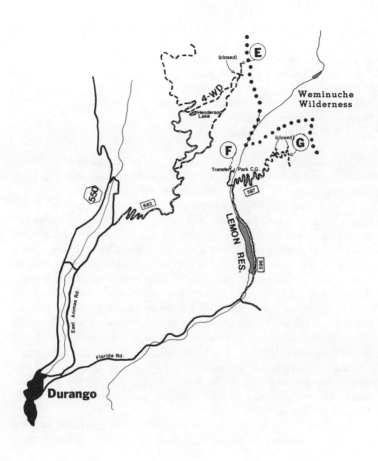

(closed)

E

4-WD

Weminuche Wilderness

Henderson Lake

(closed) **G**

F

Transfer Park C.G.

550

682

597

LEMON RES.

596

East Animas Rd.

Florida Rd.

Durango

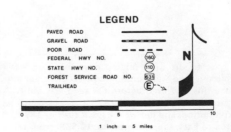

LEGEND

PAVED ROAD	
GRAVEL ROAD	
POOR ROAD	
FEDERAL HWY NO.	(160)
STATE HWY NO.	(110)
FOREST SERVICE ROAD NO.	631
TRAILHEAD	E

N

0   5   10

1 inch = 5 miles

NO. 1 — CUNNINGHAM GULCH TRAIL — — — (Trailhead A)

Trailhead elevation   —   10,440'
Total vertical ascent —   1,860'
Highest point   —   12,200'
Length   —   2.5 miles one way
Maps — 7½' Howardsville
        San Juan National Forest

        Cunningham Gulch Trail (as well as the Highland Mary Lakes
Trail) begins at the ruins of the Highland Mary Mill and is a practical way to approach the Continental Divide Trail.
        You find the Highland Mary Mill by driving north on State
Highway 110 from Silverton 4.2 miles (the first two miles are
paved) to the town site of Howardsville at the mouth of Cunningham Gulch.   Turn right onto the road up Cunningham Gulch
(Forest Service No. 589) that is squeezed in alongside the stream,
and be alert for heavy trucks since there is still some active mining.
As you drive up the gulch notice the evidence around you of the
mining of years past. At mile 2.0 from Howardsville a 4-wheel
drive road takes off to your left (Forest Service No. 737) and
climbs in 3.5 miles to Stony Pass (12,588'), the northwest end of
the Continental Divide Trail in the Weminuche Wilderness.*
Driving on straight for 2.0 more miles (you may have to stop and
throw a few rocks out of the road) brings you to the Highland
Mary Mill and the end of the road for passenger cars (elevation
10,440', trailhead A).
        About .25 mile up the jeep road you walk past another jeep
road going off to the right that goes up to the Highland Mary

---

        *In the early mining days this pass was the only way of getting to
Silverton and surrounding towns, and many people and tons of freight
came this way even before the road was built. After the Brunot Treaty was
signed with the Utes in 1873 the San Juans were opened to mining and
exploitation, and during the great rush of 1874 "Burro-packers" charged $30
a ton to pack supplies over the 12,588' pass.

Mine.** Another 500' further your road crosses Cunningham Gulch Creek. This stream will usually have to be waded. Cunningham Gulch Trail is found 10 yards or so downstream of the jeep road crossing and can be seen climbing up the hillside by the thin stands of timber. After .5 mile of steady climbing a .5 mile cut-off goes to your right to connect with the Highland Mary Lakes Trail. As you continue climbing and approach the Divide the trail levels out somewhat and you begin seeing other trails that look almost as good as yours. These trails are made by the sheep that graze in the vicinity. 1.0 mile after the cut-off to Highland Mary Lakes Trail, a grassy rounded hill about 150' high looms up directly in front of you and you can go either left or right of it to find the Continental Divide Trail (No. 59).

NO. 2 — HIGHLAND MARY LAKES TRAIL — — — (Trailhead A)

Trailhead elevation   —   10,440'
Total vertical ascent —   1,640'
Highest point   —   12,080'
Length   —   3.0 miles one way
Maps — 7½' Howardsville
        7½' Storm King Peak
        San Juan National Forest

Locate the Highland Mary Mill ruins using the approach described for trail No. 1 (trailhead A). After walking up the jeep road and crossing Cunningham Gulch Creek, stay with the road for .2 mile as it continues up the left side of the stream. The road

---

** In the 1870's a couple of brothers paid a "medium" in New York City to locate a rich mine for them. For the paltry sum of $50,000 she pointed out the present site of the Highland Mary Mine and told the brothers that a lake of gold awaited them at that spot. The spot pointed out on the map was traced to Cunningham Gulch and over $1,000,000 was invested in the shaft and a $10,000 home was built at the entrance. Silver was found but the brothers kept after the elusive lake of gold until 1885 when their funds were exhausted. In a short time, new owners developed the mine into one of the best in the area.

Read Stampede to Timberline by Muriel Sibell Wolle for more information about the mining history of Colorado and the San Juans.

becomes a trail when it enters the timber and suddenly begins to climb. Generally the trail is rocky and steep in its ascent to the lakes. Looking closely at the highly mineralized quartz outcrops tells you why the old timers were so excited about the mining potential of the area. At one point the trail wanders close to the creek and you can look at what remains of a miner's attempt to divert part of the stream from its gorge.

At 2.0 miles you cross two streams that come together a few feet below you, and it may be necessary to make these crossings with shoes and socks off. At mile 2.5 the trail enters a steep gully and climbs in or near the streambed for several hundred feet. Leaving the gully the trail goes left over a small stream, between two lakes and into the fairly level area west of the largest lake (mile 3.0).

The seven Highland Mary Lakes, in addition to Verde Lakes and Lost Lake, are grouped together in an area of about two square miles with many inter-connecting trails between them that have developed from cross-country use. About the earliest you should expect these 12,000' + lakes to be open in a normal year is around the fourth of July. These lakes are popular for the often good fishing they provide as well as their proximity to Silverton.

Camping in the vicinity of these lakes is on alpine tundra above timberline which means you will need a backpack stove and equipment that will withstand the intense storms that sometimes occur.

NO. 3 — MOLAS TRAIL — — — (Trailhead C)

Trailhead elevation   —   10,600'
Total vertical descent —   1,700'
Lowest point   —   8,900'
Length   —   4.0 miles one way
Maps — 7½' Snowdon Peak
        San Juan National Forest

The Molas Trail is a good way to beat the cost of a train ticket and visit the spectacular Elk Creek and Grenadier Range country.

The Molas Trail is found 1.25 miles down the north side of Molas Pass on Highway 550 between Durango and Silverton where a short gravel road leading to Molas Lake (not Little Molas Lake) turns east (trailhead C). About .1 of a mile down this gravel road the trail goes off to the right, beginning as vehicle tracks in the grass. Follow the tracks for about .25 mile until they curve around to the left and end in a small stand of timber. The timber is perched on the edge of a small bench and you walk about .25 mile down into a little, bare valley with a gully at the bottom. You should then begin seeing post-markers on the left side of the gully going away to the right (south) and the trail becoming clearer as you continue along. The trail does not show up on the U.S.G.S. 7½' quadrangle of the area. The trail switchbacks once to descend a bench and continues east through meadows until at mile 1.5 it enters a stand of aspen and conifers and shortly thereafter begins to switchback down to the Forest Service bridge on the Animas River. The more than thirty switchbacks are well constructed and the grade is moderate throughout. The walls of the Animas River canyon which the trail descends are very steep and you can see the Animas River and the Narrow Gauge tracks below you. A few aspen grow on the steep side and the columbine blossoms prefer this sunny, rocky slope.

After reaching the bottom of the canyon and crossing Molas Creek and the river bridge, pick up a trail which is cut into the mountain on the other side of the tracks. This trail gradually ascends (in .7 mile) to the top of the 280' bench at the beginning of Elk Creek Trail whereas if you walk down to Elk Park on the railroad tracks you would have to climb the bench in .2 mile. Not only will you have an easier ascent, but you should remember that the train discourages people from walking on the tracks (see Using the Narrow Gauge Railroad). Garfield Peak (13,074') is the impressive summit that looms over the canyon about 1.5 miles downstream on the east side.

NO.4 — ELK CREEK TRAIL

Trailhead elevation —   8,920' (Animas River bridge)
                     —   8,840' (Elk Park)
Total vertical ascent —   3,760'
Highest point   —   12,680'
Length — 9.0 miles one way
Maps — 7½' Snowdon Peak
       7½' Storm King Peak
       San Juan National Forest

Since one of the stops of the Narrow Gauge train is at Elk
Park for the Elk Creek Trail, there are prodigious amounts of
people on this trail at times. Groups such as Outward Bound and
Boy Scouts like to use Elk Creek for training grounds, and even
though there is ample camping in the "meadows" halfway up the
creek, you may find conditions a bit too crowded for comfort. Elk
Creek, like Chicago Basin, is one of those extremely beautiful and
accessible places being loved to death by people in pursuit of a
wilderness experience. If a large part of the satisfactory wilderness
experience for you is successfully finding solitude, Elk Creek in
spite of all its attractions may prove poor in this regard. September
is an excellent time for Elk Creek.

Elk Creek Trail is an old freight road built during the mining
days and has been reconstructed to serve as a hiking trail. You can
get to the Elk Creek Trail via the Molas Trail (No. 3) or as mentioned, by train. The train lets you off near a spur that goes at a
right angle to the main track for 300'. The trail begins climbing
left at the end of the spur. A steep, 280' high, aspen-covered
bench is climbed in the first .4 mile. From this point you can see
a few peaks and the first view up-canyon. The canyon is quite
narrow and at mile 1.0 you pass a pretty little waterfall that is
right on the trail. At mile 1.2 you notice a campsite that is almost
on the trail: most unsatisfactory and probably made and used by
people who were worn out after the first bench.

The trail soon begins to climb higher on the left side of the
canyon through the stands of quaking aspen. Occasionally there
are some very steep places on the trail between mile 1.5 and 3.0.
On your right (south) from the beaver ponds at mile 3.0 you can
look into Vestal Creek and to some of the spectacular peaks of

Grenadier Range. They are from left to right: Electric Peak (13,292'), Arrow Peak (13,803'), and Vestal Peak (13,664'). There is a mountaineering trail up Vestal Creek, or the "Vestal Valley" as it is called by climbers. The Grenadier Range is a seven mile long southeast-northwest line of summits, roughly parallel to Elk Creek and situated just north of the Needle Mountains. The Grenadiers were a result of some intense localized folding and faulting. In the Geological Summary of this guidebook you can read more about the geological history of Elk Creek.*

After the beaver ponds at mile 3.5 you cross a large rockslide of Precambrian rocks. Notice the size and quantity of its components. The large meadows at mile 4.0 are the destination for 9 out of every 10 Elk Creek visitors, and at an elevation of 10,200' with mountains of 13,000' bounding the valley, this is an extremely scenic place. The trail enters the timber (now the dark green of spruce and fir) and at mile 5.0 it crosses the good-sized creek that comes down from Lost Lake and Verde Lakes. You can expect to take off your shoes and socks to wade this creek in all but the driest years. The valley is narrowing fairly rapidly and at mile 5.75 the trail grows very steep and rocky. The rocks, of course, are well supplied with marmots and pikas who hurl sharp invectives as you toil upward and disturb their solitude. Before reaching an old mining cabin at mile 7.3 where the terrain levels out, the trail goes through a narrow passageway, a fault that was utilized by the makers of the trail. Elk Creek's mines were part of the Bear Creek mining district (across the Divide) and did not produce any large quantities of worthwhile ore. At the cabin the trail formerly went left to reach the Continental Divide, but you should go on straight following the little stream to find 27 switchbacks that end at the Continental Divide Trail (No. 59), elevation 12,680' (mile 9.0).

---

*For a good discussion of Elk Creek and the Grenadiers, read chapter five in Red Rock Country by Donald L. Baars, published by Doubleday Natural History Press.

NO. 5 — PURGATORY CREEK TRAIL — — — (Trailhead D)

Trailhead elevation   —   8,800'
Total vertical ascent   —   1,040'
Highest point   —   8,800'
Total vertical descent —   1,640'
Length   —   11.0 miles one way
Maps — 7½' Engineer Mountain
              7½' Electra Lake
              7½' Mountain View Crest
              San Juan National Forest

Although this trail is interesting enough in its own right, it is also an important access to the Columbine Pass Trail (No. 6) and the Needle Mountains.   Drive 28.5 miles north of Durango on Highway No. 550 and turn right into the Forest Service Purgatory Campground. The trailhead (D) can be found on the left about 20 yards in on the campground gravel road.

The trail begins dropping through a mostly aspen forest down to Purgatory Flats with a few moderately steep places here and there. Purgatory Creek (usually quite small) is crossed at mile .5 and Purgatory Flats is entered at mile 1.5, where the hiker will find an area of meadows bordered with aspen and views of the West Needle Mountains, Engineer Mountain (12,968'), Potato Hill (11,871'), and Coal Bank Hill (11,916'). Drinking from Purgatory Creek is not recommended because of development upstream.

At about mile 2.0 the trail again crosses Purgatory Creek (watch closely at this crossing because a lot of people momentarily lose their way at this point) and enters the narrow rocky gorge of Cascade Creek which is only one-half mile wide but averages over a thousand feet deep. As might be expected, there are some rock-strewn places on the trail, but it is generally in good shape. This is the sort of place where you should think ahead, and upon meeting horse parties, do your best to pass each other smoothly (see Manners on the Trail) since at times the trail is barely wide enough for two backpackers to pass and there are sheer dropoffs into the gorge. Geologically this is an interesting trail, having started in the Hermosa Formation, rocks of Pennsylvanian age, then following the Cascade Creek gorge which cuts down through Precambrian gneiss and schist as it enters the Animas River canyon.

At mile 4.5 the trail switchbacks several times and descends into the Animas River canyon (7,720') making a total drop of 1,360' over the first 5.0 miles. The trail crosses the Animas River on a Forest Service suspension bridge just below the mouth of Cascade Creek and goes over the D. & R. G. W. railroad tracks and proceeds along the Animas at the south end of the railroad bridge. The trail does not cross the railroad bridge! (Drinking from the Animas is also questionable because of discharges from the mining operations upstream in the vicinity of Silverton.) The trail here is an old wagon road, almost 100 years old, which is long since grown over and used as a pack trail. The road came from Rockwood, went up the river to Needleton (now only a few cabins), and then climbed up to Chicago Basin. Do not be put off by talk of wagon roads, railroads, and cabins. This stretch of the canyon was touched by man long ago and the effect is mainly historical today, with the railroad being the only active development at present. It's hard enough to get them to stop and pick up backpackers, so don't worry about the tourists it carries. They ride through this wild, rugged canyon as detached as someone hurrying through a museum.

Walking in the Animas Canyon is especially rewarding in June when wildflowers such as clematis, violets, and shooting stars (to name only a few) are in profusion, and the many meadows and the red-barked Ponderosa pine mixed with aspen make a delight for the eye of the observant backpacker. During the spring (spring ending sometime between May 30th and June 30th) the trail has three or four spots through which the river likes to pour, making necessary some nasty climbs through thick vegetation up the steep canyon walls. Black bears and their tracks are numerous in the canyon. If you are lucky you might spot one. Be sure to keep a clean camp (see Weather, Safety, and Wilderness Travel). At mile 5.5 fill your canteen from Crazy Woman Gulch Creek, since the next couple of miles can be quite dry and hot. The Animas canyon in this section is about two miles wide at the top and averages 3000' deep.

From about mile 8.0, you will see a couple of the many spectacular peaks in the Needle Mountains, Pigeon Peak (13,972') and Turret Peak on the right (13,835').

Needle Creek, a cold and swift-flowing stream coming from Chicago Basin, is reached at mile 11.0. Crossing the Needle Creek

bridge (8,240') and continuing for another 100 yards or so you
cross another course of Needle Creek that sometimes runs a considerable amount of water and at other times only a little. A few feet
on the other side of this are the signs directing you right to Columbine Pass Trail (No. 6) which ascends Needle Creek to Chicago
Basin.

NO. 6 — COLUMBINE PASS TRAIL

Trailhead elevation   —   8,280'
Total vertical ascent   —   4,400'
Highest point   —   12,680'
Total vertical descent   —   3,560'
Length   —   14.25 miles one way
Maps — 7½' Mountain View Crest
             7½' Columbine Pass
             San Juan National Forest

The Columbine Pass Trail which climbs Needle Creek to the
12,680' Columbine Pass and then descends Johnson Creek to
Vallecito Creek Trail (No. 10) goes through the southern end of
the Needle Mountains and within a mile of the Weminuche Wilderness' three largest peaks. I would like to remind potential users
that this is a heavy use area for two reasons: 1) the easy access by
riding the train to Needleton, and 2) the grand scenery in Chicago
Basin capped by the three 14,000' peaks. Over the 4th of July I
have seen as many as 50 or 60 people in the Basin and the number
of hikers increases every year. If you are planning a trip to the
Chicago Basin-Columbine Pass area you will have to share your
wilderness experience with quite a few other people, especially
if the time available for travel is weekends and holidays.

The trailhead for the Columbine Pass Trail is at Needle
Creek, 11.0 miles from Highway 550 via Purgatory Creek Trail
(No. 5) and trailhead (D). Or, you may ride the Narrow Gauge
Railroad to Needleton and walk .9 mile to Needle Creek and where

the trail begins.*   The trail to Columbine Pass formerly went up the creek bottom but due to the unusually violent flood of 1971, the trail has been permanently rerouted to climb the north side of Needle Creek's canyon for 1.5 miles before descending to the creek again.   Many times high waters have visited Needle Creek and the Animas River, resulting in the jumble of boulders and trees that you see along the stream beds.   The trail up Needle Creek offers only a few places where camping is convenient until the lower basin begins at about mile 4.0.   A good many people in poor physical condition attempt this trail via the train because it is well-known and a favorite in the area, and consequently you will find a lot of fire-rings perched in various cramped and narrow places on the way up.   Be prepared for a continuous and fairly steep climb (2,920' in the first 6.0 miles, and 1,480' in the last 2.0 miles), and although the late start from the train ride makes this a more difficult proposition it is still reasonably possible to make the Basin that same day if you get on with it.

At mile 2.0 or about 250 yards before you cross New York Creek, if you cross to the other side of Needle Creek, a good-sized water wheel and other interesting remnants of the mining days can be found.   This is also where you find the difficult and unmaintained manway that climbs up to Webb, Pearl, Emerald, and Ruby Lakes.   New York Creek, an attractive cascading stream, makes a refreshing cold drink and is crossed on a small bridge.   The trail continues with the same steady climb until at mile 4.0 where it begins easing into the first meadow of the lower Basin under Mount Kennedy (13,125') on your right.   Camping becomes increasingly better as you go on from this point.   As the trail levels off you begin to see the peaks that form a semi-circle at the head of Chicago Basin.   On the left is the bare, wind-swept Mount Eolus (14,083') and continuing around clockwise are Glacier Point (13,704'), Twin Thumbs, Peak 11, Needle Ridge, Sunlight Peak (14,059'), Windom Peak (14,082'), and Jupiter Mountain (13,830'). It is interesting to see the west face of Jupiter Mountain in the morning before any direct sunlight has fallen on it.   This mountain, named after the supreme god of Roman mythology, has massive godlike eyes, a nose, and a mouth from which one half expects a

---

*People who have ridden the train should add the .9 mile to the mileages given in the trail description.

Mount Kennedy (from Chicago Basin)

couple of hearty chuckles to roll across the Basin like thunder. This face is best seen not directly in front of Jupiter but from a half mile or so down the trail. Mount Eolus, across the Basin from Jupiter Mountain, is derived from mythology as well; the Homeric legends have Aeolus as appointed ruler of the winds.

The mining activity of years ago is pretty obvious to the visitor to Chicago Basin and prospects can be seen from right beside the trail to high on the side of the mountains. The "rush" was during the 80's and 90's and production from the Needles district had amounted to $200,000 by 1905. The "rush" was all but over by this time.

Walking through the meadow surrounded by the magnificent summits the trail crosses Needle Creek at mile 6.0 and begins to climb to the upper Basin and Columbine Pass. The 1,480' of climb in 2.0 miles is modified by switchbacks and after attaining the upper Basin and continuing on to the Pass (12,680') the view is very rewarding. Columbine Pass is at the head of one of the 8 to 10 glacial cirques in Chicago Basin, and a look into Johnson Creek to the east reveals an equally well-glaciated drainage. Looking straight down Johnson Creek, the obvious peaks are Organ Mountain (13,032'), with many pinnacles and spires, and Amherst Mountain (13,165'). Prominent on the left side of Johnson Creek are McCauly Peak (13,554'), and Echo Mountain (13,303'), and along the right, Florida Mountain (13,076'), and Mount Valois (13,185').

A little below Columbine Pass a rough trail goes left to reach Hazel Lake's basin (12,435') in about 1.0 miles. You will also notice a rocky trail going right and contouring along the head of the basin. This is Endlich Mesa Trail (No. 9) which reaches the 12,840' Trimble Pass in 1.6 miles. At mile 8.25 the trail levels out briefly by Columbine Lake (12,320') and traverses some very barren and scoured ground until mile 8.75 when the steep descent is resumed. After passing a few mining prospects the trail levels off at mile 10.0 where timberline is reached and good camping is possible. Johnson Creek usually doesn't have the numbers of people that are found on Needle Creek. Also, Johnson Creek averages an 11% grade, about 1% steeper than Needle Creek. At mile 10.5 the trail begins a series of switchbacks and descends steeply. Another small campsite is possible at mile 11.5. After more descent, the good-sized creek from Grizzly Gulch is crossed

at mile 13.0 and .75 later, Johnson Creek which will probably
have to be waded. At mile 14.25 there is a bridge over Vallecito
Creek and Vallecito Creek Trail (No. 10) is met.

Purgatory Creek Trail (No. 5), Columbine Pass Trail, and
Vallecito Creek Trail from mile 8.5 down to the Vallecito Campground (trailhead H) hiked in one continuous trip (33.35 miles)
take you through a great variety of scenery and elevation changes.

NO. 7 — CITY RESERVOIR — — — (Trailhead E)

Trailhead elevation   —   9,960'
Total vertical ascent   —   2,360'
Highest point   —   11,800'
Total vertical descent —   1,380'
Length   —   12.7 miles one way
(save 5.0 miles w/a 4-Wheel drive)
Maps — 7½' Mountain View Crest
        7½' Columbine Pass
        San Juan National Forest

To reach the trailhead (E) at Henderson Lake you drive
north from the Highway 550 cut-off (Trimble Lane) on East
Animas road for 3.3 miles until you reach Forest Service Missionary
Ridge Road (No. 682). This gravel road, with bone-jarring wash-
board in the first few miles, will be your route for 17.5 miles and
then turn right on a .2 mile road leading to Henderson Lake. You
then begin a walk of 5.0 miles on a road (which could be jeeped)
that will take you to the beginning of the hiking trail.* Walking .5
mile past the closure sign you then leave the road at a 90-degree
angle to the right and find several post-markers stretching across a
meadow about .4 mile wide. Look for the blazed tree at the edge
of the meadow to locate the trail and from this point it should be
fairly easy to follow. The trail goes through many beautiful stands
of dark timber (mostly Englemann spruce and subalpine fir) on the
way to City Reservoir that were saved from logging by the Wilder-

---

*Not having a 4-wheel drive vehicle I prefer to use the Florida Trail
(No. 8) which climbs 6.0 miles from the Transfer Park trailhead (F) and
meets City Reservoir Trail 1.0 mile after the end of the jeep road; much
nicer (in my opinion) than the nearly 6.0 miles of road walking through
timber sales.

ness designation. After losing a little altitude and making a couple of turns you meet the Florida Trail (No. 8) coming in from the right at mile 6.0. Continuing on, your trail crosses West Virginia Gulch at mile 7.0, a pretty little stream that wanders through pink granite with some very interesting pyrite in the stream bed.** At mile 8.5 you are descending into Virginia Gulch and you should keep left to cross closer to the head of the stream instead of taking the altitude-losing stock driveway cut-off that goes right. At the bottom of Virginia Gulch people who know the trail spread out pick it up in the timber on the other side. Look for blazes and post-markers to help you across. Climbing up you reach a divide (elevation 11,800') between Virginia Gulch and Missouri Gulch. From here the trail drops into beautiful and well-glaciated Missouri Gulch, skirts Silver Mesa to the south and at mile 12.7 meets Endlich Mesa Trail (No. 9) at Durango City Reservoir on the Florida River.

You have few encounters with other people on City Reservoir Trail because of the relatively difficult access. There is almost limitless camping in Missouri Gulch and above City Reservoir, and the gentleness of most of this country above timberline lends itself well to exploring and observations of nature. Also, this is excellent summer range for elk and sightings in the morning and evening are common.

NO. 8 — FLORIDA TRAIL — — — (Trailhead F)

Trailhead elevation   —   8,520'
Total vertical ascent —   2,080'
Highest point   —   11,600'
Length —   6.0 miles one way
Maps — 7½' Lemon Reservoir
         7½' Mountain View Crest
         San Juan National Forest

The Florida Trail ascends along the eastern side of Missionary ridge to meet City Reservoir Trail (No. 7). The opportunities for

---

**Probably not far from City Reservoir Trail is the lost "Old Florida Mine." For more information read Golden Treasures of the San Juans by Marshall and Cornelius.

campsites along this trail are limited and although there are good vistas enroute, it is used more as a means to reach the higher country than as an end in itself.

Transfer Park Campground (trailhead F) is reached by driving east from Durango on Florida Road until the Forest Service access road for Lemon Dam (No. 596) goes left. Proceed on this road and once you reach the damsite go on for 5.5 miles more and then turn left into Florida Campground. Drive on through and go 1.5 miles more to the Transfer Park Campground. The trail begins in a small meadow where the road swings to the right just before entering the campground.

Even though you walk through some clear-cutting, the Florida Trail is enjoyable to hike because of the transition through different life zones. Starting from what is almost a "foothills" environment with Ponderosa pine, some oakbrush and Douglas fir, the trail progresses through a belt of aspen from about 9,000' to 10,000' and ends in the spruces and firs of the sub-alpine zone. Despite the fact that the trail originates from the vicinity of Lemon Dam, an area well known by vacationers, you rarely meet hikers after the first mile or two.

The trail is easy to follow at first and climbs 1,000' in 1.5 miles. At this point South Burnt Timber Creek is crossed and you should keep your eyes open for grouse. At mile 2.0 you are on the edge of a large meadow that climbs to the top of Missionary Ridge and here the trail crosses Burnt Timber Creek. The trail is unclear and overgrown. You can lose a few feet of elevation and find some switchbacks in the aspen on the other side of the creek. Or, you can continue up the left side of Burnt Timber Creek for another .2 mile before crossing. The trails come together in the meadows as you reach a bench (mile 3.0) where views of the peaks and mesas around Durango City Reservoir are very good. The trail contours through North Burnt Timber Creek and then climbs up to meet an old and closed logging road. This road climbs almost immediately but you keep right with a poorer one that contours into a level logged area. The U.S.G.S. map is incorrect here as it shows the trail staying with the better road the rest of the way. The trail can be seen fairly well through here and at the end of the clear-cut where steep-forested walls lie ahead of you, cross a little stream at mile 4.75, angle left, and find the trail making some eroded switchbacks to the benches above. At mile

6.0 you meet City Reservoir Trail (No. 7).

NO. 9 — ENDLICH MESA TRAIL — — — (Trailhead G)

Trailhead elevation   —   11,280'
Total vertical ascent —   3,243'
Highest point   —   12,840'
Total vertical descent —   1,803'
Length — 13.0 miles one way
Maps — 7½' Lemon Reservoir
       7½' Vallecito Reservoir
       7½' Columbine Pass
       San Juan National Forest

The access road for Endlich Mesa Trail is long, at the end poor, and the trail is hard to find. The section of the trail that receives the most use is from Durango City Reservoir to Columbine Pass. At mile 6.5 Endlich Mesa Trail is met by City Reservoir Trail (No. 7) and this is the way you should go if you don't read maps well.

You find your way to Lemon Reservoir as described in trail No. 8 but at 5.5 miles up the road from the damsite you should go straight on the East Florida Road (No. 597). This logging road climbs for 9.5 miles to a road closure (trailhead G); the last three or four miles might not be passable for passenger cars in wet weather. After the closure sign you walk on the main road as it climbs past other side roads. At mile 1.0 from the closure when you see the logging road ahead of you cutting into a steep hillside that is the ridgetop, you must go left through a small clearing to find the trail in the timber at the top of the ridge. This is a real difficult trail to locate and you should use the U.S.G.S. 7½' quadrangle which shows the East Florida Road and where the trail takes off from it.

At mile 1.5 you break out of the timber and ascend a small hill. When you descend the somewhat steeper north end of the hill to a saddle, you must watch closely since a game trail that goes off to the left is obvious but you have to keep right and maintain a northeasterly direction of travel. You will see your trail clearly in 100 yards or less.

The confusing and ambigious part is now over and the trail is easily followed from this point on. Your reward for persistence is walking on top of the world (or so it seems) across the alpine tundra of Endlich Mesa,* which averages 12,000' high for over 2.0 miles. Across the Florida River to the west is Missionary Ridge and behind that the La Plata Mountains. North you can see some of the rugged Needle Mountains and east through breaks in the rim of the mesa you can look down to Vallecito Reservoir about 4,500' below.

Finally at mile 4.5 the trail goes through a saddle, drops into a basin and stays near the head of it until at mile 5.0 where it climbs a narrow ridge. Sheridan Mountain (12,795') dominates the view as you look across the next basin. This is a good place to study the headwaters of the Florida River. Notice that Missouri Gulch and the valleys above City Reservoir are perfect examples of straightening done by glacial ice. You have a good view of Silver Mesa as it rises to almost 13,000' toward the Needle Mountains between Missouri Gulch and Crystal Valley on the right.

From the narrow ridge the trail turns right to descend and after about 150 yards, it turns down a draw and soon enters the timber. At 5.75 you cross the unnamed creek that begins on the flank of Sheridan Mountain. Contouring around a ridge you come to the valley of the Florida River. Here the trail crosses the primitive dam of Durango City Reservoir** and meets City Reservoir Trail (No. 7) on the left. Continuing around the lake you will find camping space at the upper end. As with all high altitude lakes the fishing at Durango City Reservoir (10,917') is variable but the lake contains some fine fish. North of the lake the trail climbs steeply through thin stands of timber until at mile 8.0 you reach the 11,555' Lake Marie. Beaver have assisted the development of this body of water. The site of the mining community of Logtown, which had mail delivery and served the mining interests in the area during the 1880's is along the Florida River from Lake Marie to about .2 mile below it. You can still find a few trimmed logs at

---

*Named after Frederick Endlich, a geologist with the Hayden Survey party who explored here in the 1870's.

**The headwaters of the Florida River including Durango City Reservoir, Lake Marie, Lillie Lake and Castilleja Lake are part of a 2,800-acre reservoir grant made in the 1880's to assure the city of Durango a good water supply.

this location.

Almost even with the lake the trail switches back and climbs the side of Silver Mesa. Silver Mesa is alpine tundra and dotted with small lakes and a few prospects by miners. The trail is marked by rock cairns. At mile 10.3 you go close by the ruins of the Pittsburg Mine*** and at mile 11.4 you reach Trimble Pass (12,840'). Before you cross Trimble Pass you can see Lillie Lake (12,550') contained in a tight basin below Florida Mountain (13,076'). The rock-filled trail over to Columbine Pass (12,680'), mile 13.0, is slow going but the view is superb as you make your way around the head of Johnson Creek below Bullion Mountain (13,182').

***In 1881 the mine excited enough interest to warrant a considerable investment. During 1884, 50 tons of ore were shipped to Denver. The operation was abandoned, though, at the end of the summer, because of the expense of sending ore out for smelting and shipping supplies in by packhorse.

II.
Vallecito Creek
and the Pine River

	trailhead	length
No. 10 — Vallecito Creek Trail	(H)	17.0 miles
No. 11 — Rock Creek Trail		7.5 miles
No. 12 — Dollar Lake Trail	(I)	5.25 miles
No. 13 — Hell Canyon Trail (manway)		3.0 miles
No. 14 — Pine River Trail	(J)	22.0 miles
No. 15 — Emerald Lake Trail		8.75 miles
No. 16 — Half Moon Trail (manway)		2.0 miles
No. 17 — Flint Creek Trail		7.0 miles
No. 18 — Sierra Vandera Creek Trail (manway)		10.0 miles
No. 19 — Divide Lakes Trail		1.8 miles
No. 20 — Granite Lake Trail		1.0 miles
No. 21 — Snowslide Canyon Trail		4.0 miles
No. 22 — Rincon La Osa Trail		6.0 miles

95.3 miles

The Vallecito and Pine River drainages are extensive and penetrate the Wilderness at its widest. Vallecito Creek Trail climbs to the Continental Divide at the eastern end of the Needle Mountains and is very spectacular and well-known. A group of mountains east of Vallecito Creek and north of Emerald Lake could be called the Eastern Needles because of their similar appearance and height.

The Pine River valley traverses a somewhat gentler but equally beautiful section of the Wilderness to reach the Divide and has many trails originating from it. Emerald, Moon, Flint, and Rock Lakes are approachable from these trails and are popular destinations for fishermen. The Pine River Trail is extensively used by horsemen, commercial and otherwise. Despite the large numbers of people, the size of this section is great and many fine places can be found to "get away from it all."

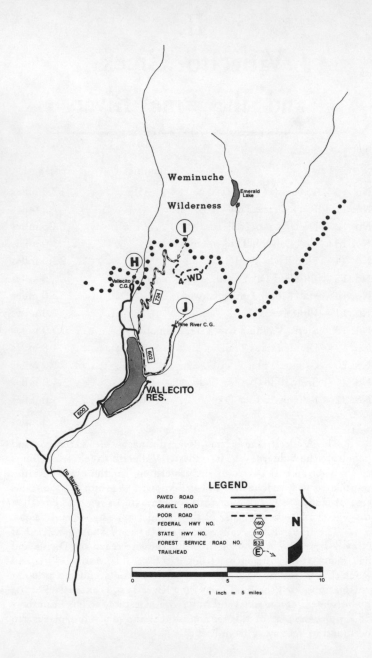

Weminuche

Wilderness

Emerald
Lake

(I)

(H)

4-WD

Vallecito
C.G.

724

(J)

Pine River C.G.

603

VALLECITO
RES.

600

(to Bayfield)

LEGEND

PAVED ROAD	
GRAVEL ROAD	
POOR ROAD	
FEDERAL HWY NO.	(160)
STATE HWY NO.	(110)
FOREST SERVICE ROAD NO.	631
TRAILHEAD	(E)

N

0   5   10

1 inch = 5 miles

NO. 10 — VALLECITO CREEK TRAIL — — — (Trailhead H)

Trailhead elevation   —   7,916'
Total vertical ascent —   3,604'
Highest point   —   11,520'
Length — 17.0 miles one way
Maps — 7½' Vallecito Reservoir
         7½' Columbine Pass
         7½' Storm King Peak
         San Juan National Forest

Vallecito (Spanish: little valley) Creek Trail, one of the most scenic in the Wilderness, begins at the Vallecito Creek Campground (H). To reach Vallecito Reservoir you can go north from Highway 160 at Bayfield on the paved county road known as the Vallecito Road, or east from Durango on paved Florida Road. When you reach the dam it is another 5.0 miles to the Vallecito Forest Service Work Center, where you go left at a junction for 3.0 more miles to the trailhead at Vallecito Campground.

Vallecito Trail is one of the most heavily used trails in the Weminuche Wilderness. Many people take the Narrow Gauge Train to Needleton and climb to Columbine Pass, descend Johnson Creek to Vallecito Trail and go out to Vallecito Campground. Another popular route is to ascend Vallecito Trail to Rock Creek and from here go over the Pine River Trail (No. 14) via Rock Creek Trail (No. 11) and Flint Creek Trail (No. 17). Vallecito Trail below Johnson Creek takes on the appearance of a super highway and it is not uncommon to meet forty or more people a day in mid-summer.

.6 mile after beginning there is a very spectacular gorge through which Vallecito Creek makes a noisy passage while the trail hangs on cliffs 400' above. This cliff area is dangerous for horses, so make all encounters as smooth as possible (see Manners on the Trail). On the granite along the trail you can see rocks smoothed by glacial action. North you should be able to view Irving Peak (13,218'), a classic-looking mountain that is framed by the valley ahead. The trail eases off the cliffs and at mile 3.0 you cross Taylor Creek and then Vallecito Creek with the first of three bridges. The little park at Taylor Creek has received quite a bit of use so get an early enough start so you won't have to stop here overnight and add your bit too. By July the vegetation along the

Irving Peak (center) above Vallecito Creek Valley.

trail is almost tropical from here up to the next two bridges. Green gentian, which grow to over six feet tall, thimbleberry bushes, solomonseal, columbine, and daisies are some of the larger, more obvious flowers. But take the time to look closer to the ground and you will see the minute violets, purple and yellow, and other tiny blossoms. Also seen along this trail is the very rare red lily. Please enjoy these flowers without picking them.

At mile 5.2 the second bridge takes the trail to the west side of the narrow valley and at mile 6.5 you cross the Soda Spring hanging bridge. The valley now changes dramatically* to meadows with aspen climbing the mountainsides. Quite a few small streams descend from the mountainsides and cross the expansive meadows on their way to Vallecito Creek. At mile 7.5 you enter a small stand of spruce and cross Irving Creek, the largest of these streams. A little ways further a strong trail goes left to an outfitter's camp but you keep right, and soon you meet Columbine Pass Trail (No. 6) where it crosses the Vallecito on a bridge at mile 8.5. West you see some of the impressive summits of the Needle Mountains with Thunder Mountain (13,108') being the most prominent. This is good country for elk, deer, black bear, and bighorn sheep, but these big game animals are shy and stay well away from the trails. As you continue up the creek the grade increases somewhat, big Vallecito Creek begins to roar and the valley seems almost arched by the summits that tower 3,000' on either side. Roell Creek, whose headwaters are in the nearly inaccessible Hidden and Lost Lakes, is extremely cold and may have to be waded. About .5 mile above Roell the U.S.G.S. map shows a crossing of the Vallecito. The trail only divides and it is not necessary to cross to continue. When you enter the meadows across from Sunlight Creek you will notice that a scenic campsite is possible here. The mountain to the west is Vallecito Mountain (13,428'). After a section of forest the trail breaks into meadows across from Leviathan Creek at mile 12.7, not very suitable for camping. Sunlight Creek, Leviathan Creek and the yet to come Stormy Gulch (mile 15.5) have manways ascending them that have developed from countless climbing parties going into the Needles.

---

*The Ute Indians loved to hunt and roam the Vallecito and Pine River high country. It is said that the first white men to enter the upper Vallecito found many sweat lodges (Indian saunas) of the Utes along the stream.

At the mile 14.0 you cross the reddish-colored Rock Creek**
and the Rock Creek Trail (No. 11) goes right just after crossing the
stream. Expect to take off shoes and socks for this one. An impressive mountain, The Guardian (13,617'), hangs over the valley to
the west. Be sure to look down-canyon from the vicinity of Rock
Creek because the view into the Needles is very fine. The area
around Rock Creek is heavily used and you might have difficulty
in finding a place to pitch your tent at certain times.

Continuing on, the valley narrows down and at mile 15.5 you
look up Stormy Gulch to Mt. Silex (13,628'), north of The Guardian, and Storm King Peak (13,752'), to the right of Mt. Silex. The
trail has some muddy places as you go through the timber after the
Stormy Gulch vista and you may have to ford still another creek.
Nebo Creek is really a delight to watch, though, as it cascades over
rocks and away from the trail. After crossing an unnamed tributary of Nebo Creek that comes from Hunchback Pass, you meet the
Continental Divide Trail (No. 59) at mile 17.0, 1.5 miles from
Nebo Pass and 1.5 miles from Hunchback Pass.

NO. 11 — ROCK CREEK TRAIL

Trailhead elevation   —   10,133'
Total vertical ascent   —   3,187'
Highest point   —   12,000'
Total vertical descent —   400'
Length   —   7.5 miles one way
Maps — 7½' Storm King Peak
          7½' Emerald Lake
          7½' Rio Grande Pyramid
          San Juan National Forest

Rock Creek Trail begins at mile 14.0 on Vallecito Creek Trail
(No. 10). The lakes on the hydrological divide between Flint and
Rock Creeks, as well as the accessibility of the Ute Lakes country
just over the Continental Divide, are primary reasons for the heavy

---

**From where the mineralized springs seep into Rock Creek to about
1.0 mile down the Vallecito there are no fish. For drinking, the water seems
fine but for extended use it might be better to be on the safe side and take
water from the Vallecito above Rock Creek.

use this area receives. Also, Rock Creek Trail and Flint Creek Trail connect the Vallecito and Pine River Trails and this is a popular way of crossing from one drainage to the other.

The first 1.5 miles of trail climb a little over 1000′ to where the large meadows begin. The meadows make good pictures but poor camping because of bogs and springs and the better camping is at the upper end of these meadows around mile 3.0. After the meadows, when you start to climb and ford Rock Creek at mile 3.5, a trail takes off left. This is one of the many non-Forest Service trails in the vicinity you will find to bewilder you. Generally these trails cause erosion because they are poorly situated and are the result of an outfitter's repeated use of a time saving cut-off, practical only for one direction of travel. You stay right and again wade Rock Creek at mile 3.75. Just before crossing Rock Creek at this point a .2 mile trail ascends the creek on the right to 11,841′ Rock Lake. If you plan on camping at this good-sized lake (31 acres) tucked away in a glacial cirque, make sure you have the kind of equipment necessary to weather storms and cook above timberline. Behind and to the right of Rock Lake is Peters Peak (13,122′), and standing watch over Rock Creek is the hump-backed Buffalo Peak (12,728′). Around the lake to the east a manway (No. 16) begins and climbs over the mountains to Half Moon and Moon Lakes.

Back on Rock Creek Trail, you curve left under an 800′ cliff with icy cold springs at the base and climb a few switchbacks. At mile 4.4 you will meet a short trail which climbs 320′ to the Continental Divide, which at this point is a grass covered slope. The Continental Divide Trail (No. 59) is .8 mile away and Twin Lakes (on the Ute Creek drainage) are 1.5 miles distant. You keep right and lose a little elevation as you pass some of the small lakes of the Flint Lakes group. You will also notice some very rough country to the south (right) with many unnamed peaks deeply gouged with glacial cirques that contain quite a few lakes and no trails.

At mile 5.5 Flint Creek Trail (No. 17) is met coming in from the right and Rock Creek Trail turns left and passes by the big Flint Lake (11,620′), about 300′ away. This attractive lake has a shoreline with boulders and trees right to the water's edge and looks as though it could have come from the north woods of Minnesota. After meandering through some glacially well-polished bedrock country the trail comes to a little valley at mile 6.8 which you ascend until you meet the Continental Divide Trail (No. 59) at mile 7.5.

NO. 12 — DOLLAR LAKE TRAIL — — — (Trailhead I)

Trailhead elevation   —   10,640'
Total vertical ascent   —   1,840'
Highest point   —   12,320'
Total vertical descent   —   160'
Length   —   5.25 miles one way
Maps — 7½' Vallecito Reservoir
             7½' Emerald Lake
             San Juan National Forest

     This trail is not on any but the guidebook maps for the first 3.0 miles. However, anyone who wishes to visit Dollar Lake and vicinity should go this way. The U.S.G.S. and Forest Service maps show a trail beginning from mile 11.0 on the Middle Mountain Road, which is difficult to find and once enroute, easy to lose. The logging road that leads to the trailhead is found by driving to the Forest Service Vallecito Work Center as described in trail No. 10. After keeping right from the junction for 1.0 mile you find Middle Mountain Road (No. 724) going left and climbing 10.0 miles to the trailhead (I). Middle Mountain Road is not for cars with low clearance and the last two miles may be bad in wet weather. Mile 10.0 is the last curve that crosses the South Fork of Bear Creek before the road reaches the gate on the ridgetop, mile 11.0, the trailhead shown on all but the guidebook's map.

     You leave your car at the curve and climb through a logged area. The road (be sure to stay with the main one) switchbacks three times and about 20 yards after the third switchback you see a trail climbing steeply away to the right. It is still in the cut area, however, and hard to follow as it crosses the tip of another switchback and soon enters the trees. The trail is headed for a saddle on the ridge and reaches this point at mile 1.2. The trail has become very clear as it goes left of a tree with a gray Wilderness boundary sign. The trail now travels along the east side of a ridge and there is little water for drinking. At mile 1.8 you walk through a meadow and then at mile 2.8 you enter a larger meadow from which you can look down to the pleasant meadows and forest of Cave Basin. The trail fades for a moment when you are passing an isolated tree-covered hill which is on the right, but keep going in the direction the trail was taking and you will find it again. After more easy walking, at about mile 3.5 you will be above timberline and on tundra. The few trees you see are grotesquely twisted and lie close to the ground to take advantage of the cover of winter snows and get protection from the dry, piercing cold winter winds. Only hints and fragments of the trail will be found the rest of the way to Dollar Lake. From this high rolling country there are incredible views northwest into the Needle Mountains. You should see a huge rock cairn after walking cross-country for .5 mile. Your line of travel then swings more northeast (right) toward the mountains which are met by the abruptly rising plateau on which you are walking. Just before the first mountain you find Dollar Lake (mile 5.25) in a cirque with the waters of Emerald Lake visible in the valley below. No trail descends to Dollar Lake so you have the choice of making your way down to the south or north side. The south side is less steep but has some sliderock while the north is steeper but has more grassy slopes. There is very little camping space around Dollar Lake and camping on the tundra above would require equipment able to withstand the full force of storms.

The vicinity of Dollar Lake could be the beginning for a mountaineering trip into the rough unnamed summits above 13,000' that lie ahead of you around Mt. Oso.

NO. 13 — HELL CANYON TRAIL (Manway)

Trailhead elevation   —   9,200'
Total vertical ascent —   2,360'
Highest point   —   11,650'
Length —   3.0 miles one way
Maps — 7½' Emerald Lake
       San Juan National Forest

This appropriately named trail is steep, very deteriorated, covered with huge blow-downs of timber impossible to traverse and it ends in a vague way near Dollar Lake Trail (No. 12) in Cave Basin. You won't see any other people here but you will probably

wish you weren't here either. There is no camping enroute. The
trail is found 2.0 miles up Emerald Lake Trail where it crosses
Lake Creek into a small tilted meadow. The guidebook's map
shows this manway as accurately as possible and no other description will be given. This trail is not recommended for travel.

NO. 14 — PINE RIVER TRAIL — — — (Trailhead J)

Trailhead elevation   —   7,910'
Total vertical ascent —   2,720'
Highest point   —   10,630'
Length — 22.0 miles one way
Maps — 7½' Vallecito Reservoir
         7½' Granite Peak
         7½' Emerald Lake
         7½' Granite Lake
         7½' Weminuche Pass
         San Juan National Forest

To reach the Pine River Campground, the trailhead (J) for
the Pine River Trail, you drive to the Vallecito Forest Service Work
Center as described in trail No. 10. You keep right at this junction
and continue for 7.2 miles to the Pine River Campground.

The Pine River (also called Los Pinos) Trail goes through
the heart of the Wilderness and it meets or is the trailhead for
eleven other trails. This generally wide, clear trail has few steep
places which makes it a favorite with horse packers. Although
this trail receives heavy use particularly up to Flint Creek Trail
(No. 17), mile 11.75, the valley is large, and camping with a certain
amount of solitude is usually available, especially in the upper
half. Commercial horse packers don't have a big impact until July
and the lower elevations of the Pine can provide some fine snow-
free hiking. The trail stays on the west side of the Pine River the
entire way, avoiding what would be a pretty rough crossing from
La Osa Creek on down.

The Pine River Trail ends at Weminuche Pass (10,622'),
the lowest point on the Continental Divide in the Weminuche
Wilderness. This fact in addition to the gentle ascent made the
valley a natural for the Indian-engineered trail that the first explorers found. It is also said that buffalo roamed across spacious

Weminuche Pass.

The trail is on private land for the first 5.0 miles and the fences and gates are aesthetically inappropriate for the beginning of this important trail. The Forest Service plans to negotiate permanent right-of-way for this section but until that time please obey all signs and avoid actions which might encourage the Granite Peak Ranch to close the access. The trail passes through the nearly level valley with large old Ponderosa pines mixed with Douglas fir and occasional white fir trees. Watch for the beautiful tasscl-eared (Abert) squirrel around the Ponderosas. At mile 1.25 you cross Indian Creek, where you can stop for a cold drink on the sometimes dusty trail. At mile 2.5 you look up over 3,000' of rockslide to Runlett Peak (11,188'), where you will probably be watched by marmots who live in this heap of lichen-covered boulders. Continuing on, the way is a wildflower enthusiast's delight. Low places along the trail are boggy which makes perfect conditions for such beauties as purple monkshood, bog orchids, larkspur, arnica, and thick bushy growths of bluebells. After about mile 3.0 you can look across the valley to Granite Peak (12,147'), but you cannot see the actual summit. You cross a bridge at Lake Creek (mile 5.75) and this is a good lunch stop where you can watch the waters coming from Emerald and Moon Lakes. In about 150 yards, Emerald Lake Trail (No. 15) goes left along with many of the people. The valley walls close in for the next 2.0 miles and the Pine River thunders through the narrow granite channel below you. If you take off your pack and work your way down into the gorge, there are marvelous cascades, chutes and falls on this wild river that can fascinate you for hours. The valley widens briefly at mile 7.5 for a good campsite* in an aspen grove and then narrows until a little past mile 8.0, at Willow Park. From Willow Park (about 8,720'), aspen becomes the tree that dominates the

---

*There were improved campsites with table, grates and outhouses at Blue Spruce Canyon, Willow Park, Falls Creek, Flag Mountain and around Emerald Lake until they were removed in the summer of 1975 after the area received Wilderness designation.

scenery**.

The river meanders through this spacious valley and at mile
9.0 there is a large double falls on Falls Creek to the right. Porcu-
pine Creek, which is at mile 10.5, runs quite a bit of water and may
have to be forded in the early season. You begin to gain some
elevation as you climb to Flint Creek and Flint Creek Trail (No.
17), mile 11.75. Before you leave the hillside turn around and
look down-canyon; there is almost a text-book example of a U-
shaped glacial valley laid out before you. To the east is rough Flag
Mountain (12,323').

When you are removing your shoes and socks to cross cold
Flint Creek, look up Flint Creek canyon to the unusual rock formation of Pope's Nose (11,148'). The trail crosses Flint Creek in a
good place, but a third leg in the form of a sturdy stick may be
helpful. You now encounter the part of the Pine River Trail that
has any real steepness and about .5 mile past Flint Creek there is
a tremendous falls on the Pine a short way down from the trail.
Sierra Vandera Creek is soon seen where it joins the Pine from the
east. Climbing through the thick aspen forest you cross a number
of small streams including Pope Creek (mile 13.0) which is well
utilized by a beaver colony***. .2 mile further on is where you
would make a difficult crossing of the Pine to reach Sierra Vandera
Trail (No. 18; also called the Pine-Piedra Driveway). After another
.5 mile the valley opens up and levels out once more. The
character of the land changes because soon the light colored aspen
are left behind for the dark spruces and firs. The trail looks like
it crosses the Pine here but you can stay with a trail high on the
left to avoid this.

At mile 14.4 you have to cross South Canyon Creek and if
the run-off is heavy you may have to make still another ford. The
valley may be at its prettiest in this section with grassy benches

---

**Records show that around the turn of the century, and just before
the National Forest was organized, there were quite a few fires along the
Pine River and Vallecito drainages that burned extensive acreages. Although
this is the normal elevation for aspen it is probable that the way for them
was cleared by these disastrous fires.

***The beaver was nearly trapped out of existence in the Rocky
Mountains by the mountain men in the 19th century. Beavers have made a
remarkable comeback and the Forest Service and the Game and Fish Department even have to restrict their activities at Pope Creek in order to maintain
a trail.

extending out to the slow-moving river. Camping on one of these benches can reward you with sights such as a beaver making his way upriver or a red-tailed hawk keeping his country under surveillance. At mile 15.5 you pass the Granite Peak Guard Station, built in 1916 for Wilderness management. .3 mile further, you are across from an opening in the valley wall to the east where Divide Lakes are located and Divide Lakes Trail (No. 19) and Granite Lake Trail (No. 20) begin. You cross, and will possibly have to wade Cañon Paso at mile 16.6. The trail climbs a little more now, through some muddy places. At mile 18.25 there is a cut-off that crosses the Pine to a good camping place at the mouth of Snowslide Canyon. The Piedra Stock Driveway (No. 23), which passed the east side of Granite Lake, is also found in these concealed meadows .5 mile east of the Pine River. Before Rincon La Osa you begin to hear, then see a miniature Niagara Falls on the Pine River, and shortly thereafter, at mile 19.0 you come to Rincon La Osa Trail (No. 22). It will be necessary to wade La Osa Creek. Climbing 350' in the next mile, you top a hill and see the two-mile long by ½-mile wide meadows of Weminuche Pass laid out before you. This has to be one of the most beautiful places in the Weminuche Wilderness with the steep mountainsides rising from the vast expanse of meadow. At mile 20.8 after crossing (and probably fording) Rincon La Vaca Creek you meet the Continental Divide Trail (No. 59) as it crosses the valley to the east to ascend the North Fork of the Pine. It may be hard to see at this point. Also, from this position you should be able to get a view of the Rio Grande Pyramid and La Ventana (the Window) to the west, two important landmarks for explorers. At mile 21.1 you cross a diversion ditch**** and find the Continental Divide Trail going west up La Vaca Creek. Continue north and at mile 22.0 you arrive at Weminuche Pass (10,622')***** and can take Weminuche Creek Trail (No. 53) down to Rio Grande Reservoir and Thirty-

----

****The Raber Lohr Ditch, taking water from Rincon La Vaca Creek, and the Fuchs Ditch, taking water from the North Fork of the Pine, were built in 1935 and ease western slope waters over gentle Weminuche Pass to the Rio Grande and arid San Luis Valley.

*****James Pattie was probably the first white to cross Weminuche Pass. Directed up the Pine River by Utes who were camped in the vicinity of the present site of Bayfield, the passage took six days, in early May 1827, and his personal narrative speaks of bare peaks and compact snow drifts higher than a man on a horse.

Mile Campground (BB) or the high La Vaca trail that climbs up in the old burn to the west (left).

NO. 15 — EMERALD LAKE TRAIL

Trailhead elevation   —   8,360'
Total vertical ascent —   3,260'
Highest point   —   11,620'
Length —   8.75 miles one way
Maps — 7½' Emerald Lake
             San Juan National Forest

The destination of many visitors to the Pine River country of the Weminuche Wilderness is magnificent Emerald Lake. Emerald Lake is 4.0 miles up Emerald Lake Trail and is noted for its size (second largest natural lake in Colorado at 279 acres), its scenic beauty and good fishing. This mile and a half long by ½ mile wide, 248' deep, landslide-created lake has fairly adequate camping along the east side and usually not high numbers of people around the middle of the week. Beware of the hordes around the 4th of July, though. Even in times of heavy use you can usually find a secluded campsite a mile or so above the lake. Dry, warm winters have seen Emerald Lake (10,033') open by Memorial Day, but the average date is closer to the middle of June.

Emerald Lake Trail begins on the Pine River Trail (No. 14) at mile 5.75. The well-marked trail ascends steeply at first through aspen and conifers with vociferous Lake Creek not far away. The walls of Lake Creek's canyon tower 3,000' above you. At mile 1.5 the trail levels off into a meadow called the "cabbage patch" which is full of miner's candles. If you have walked from the Pine River Campground you may be eyeing this area as a campsite. It is not too satisfactory and there are a few small sites closer to Lake Creek a little further on. You may be asked to move by the Forest Service anyway. Another small meadow and at mile 2.0 you are right by Lake Creek where Hell Canyon Manway (No. 13) crosses. The U.S.G.S. map shows your trail briefly crossing here but you don't have to worry; it doesn't. You soon begin the steep climb that will

take you over the landslide that formed Emerald Lake*. At mile
3.0 you reach an area where the trees thin out to some small and
twisted aspen. This is a snowslide path which runs over the old
landslide and is a very good place for wildflowers. Scattered
among the rocks you find flowers that prefer a sunny well-drained
slope: showy daisies, purple and yellow, Indian paintbrush, and
harebells, to name a few.

Entering a stand of dark timber which often contains snow
into July, you slowly climb over the crest of the landslide and
descend to Little Emerald Lake. The trail picks its way through
gigantic boulders and at mile 4.0 you come to a junction in the
trail. Left takes you between Big and Little Emerald Lakes and to
some breezy campsites. Right, you continue along the east shoreline of Big Emerald, to the meadows in the valley above and eventually to Moon Lake. When you reach Emerald Lake you will
notice a noisy falls on the opposite side of the lake. The water
comes down from Dollar Lake and usually tapers off by mid-
summer. The route around Emerald is almost continually climbing
or descending small amounts and the paths of several snowslides
that go right into the lake are crossed. The snowslides leave the
slopes clear for beautiful flower gardens. In July you may be able
to identify 15 — 20 different kinds of flowers growing in these
spots. At mile 5.5 at the end of the lake a small stream is crossed
and after another .2 mile you will have to ford Lake Creek, a very
full stream until late summer.

Climbing moderately on the west side of Lake Creek through
the upper valley, you will find many meadows along the capricious
stream. Spectacular falls plunge down from hidden cirques and the
grandeur of the setting is enhanced by the fine unnamed peaks at
the head of the valley. At mile 7.0 you cross Lake Creek again
and shortly thereafter the way grows steep. The canyon curves
left and as you climb past many cold streams that beg to be sam-
pled, you will soon see a big falls on Lake Creek and also one on a
tributary of Lake Creek to the left. After more hard climbing, the
trail levels into the area below the most spectacular falls on Lake

---

*Geologists believe that the landslide of Precambrian granite tumbled
into the valley from the east side. The depth and sheerness of the walls
created by intense glaciation were the conditions that helped bring about
this massive slide.

Emerald Lake

Creek's drainage. At mile 8.5 you cross Lake Creek again and climb the remaining .25 mile to Moon Lake (11,620'). This fair-sized lake with a highly curved shoreline has a manway (No. 16) around the north side (right) that ascends to Half Moon Lake and over the mountains to Rock Lake. Mt. Oso (13,684') is the large dominating summit to the west.

NO. 16 — HALF MOON TRAIL (Manway)

Trailhead elevation   —   11,841'
Total vertical ascent —   639'
Highest point   —   12,480'
Total vertical descent —   860'
Length —   2.0 miles one way
Maps — 7½' Emerald Lake
          San Juan National Forest

This manway, which connects Rock Creek Trail (No. 11) and Emerald Lake Trail (No. 15) has developed from the cross-country route between Rock and Moon Lakes. Since it is narrow and rocky, you have to pick your way carefully because this would be a poor place to get a sprained ankle.

From Rock Lake you walk around the east side, climb the low hills and locate a steep gully of grass and rock. This gully leads to a small valley that runs east under the face of an unnamed 13,120' peak. As you work up the gully you begin seeing small cairns consisting of two or three rocks and soon the trail becomes evident. The gully levels out and you turn right before reaching a little rock-bound lake. Be sure you locate the cairns that mark the trail as you begin the steep ascent to the saddle that lies ahead. As you climb through the sliderock it appears that rocks have been rolled aside in the worst places to improve the trail. When you reach the saddle at mile .75 you must immediately turn right and climb another 80' of elevation. This bypasses some dangerous cliffs you would encounter if you begin traversing from the low point of the saddle.

You are in a world of mostly rock, angling steeply skyward. The view down to Moon Lake and the mountains around it is breathtaking. This would be a likely place to observe ptarmigan.

The route circles left to a small grassy basin and the obvious

trail that descends to Half Moon Lake (12,200') at mile 1.0. There
is no satisfactory camping at Half Moon Lake. The trail begins to
descend from Half Moon's basin and crosses to the left side of the
stream. The way is rocky and slow-going until it levels out somewhat. You then go right (the cairns are now scarce) and the stream
is recrossed just before the final steepness above Moon Lake's
basin. Walking along the north shoreline you cross the lake's outlet
and find Emerald Lake Trail (No. 15).

If you want to go from Moon Lake to Rock Lake be sure
that summer is far enough along so that the snow is at a minimum.
You could easily ascend the sunny south slopes from Moon and
Half Moon Lakes and then have difficulties with snow on the
north faces above Rock Lake. Generally, this route is not practical
for the average backpacker until the middle of July.

NO. 17 — FLINT CREEK TRAIL

Trailhead elevation   —   9,200'
Total vertical ascent —   2,440'
Highest point   —   11,640'
Length   —   7.0 miles one way
Maps — 7½' Emerald Lake
              San Juan National Forest

Flint Creek Trail begins at mile 11.75 on the Pine River Trail
(No. 14). This is a heavily used trail and, in places, is rutted one to
two feet deep. Flint Creek Trail is well-known because of Flint
and Rock Lakes (see trail No. 11) located in the scenic high country where Flint Creek begins. Also, Flint Creek Trail is the first
opportunity along the Pine River Trail where the mountains may
be crossed (via Flint Creek Trail, then Rock Creek Trail, No. 11)
and Vallecito Trail (No. 10) reached. It is likely that you will
encounter a good many horse packers on this trail.

The trail is well marked where it leaves the Pine River Trail
and here at the beginning, in the meadows on both sides of the
creek, are some nice areas for camping. In the first part of summer
the violets growing here seem to be unsurpassed in their deep
purple color. Soon the trail is climbing and on the right good-sized
Flint Creek is very lively. The smoothed granite walls high on your
right (north) show the effects of the glacier that occupied this

canyon as it ground down to the main valley. About mile 1.2 you are below the 11,148' Pope's Nose, an ethnic slur preserved for posterity, and here you find a few small campsites by the creek. At mile 1.6 you are in rocky Barebottom Park (9,560'), which is sloping and unsuitable for an overnight stay. As you continue up Flint Creek, the trail is characterized by short sections of moderately steep climbing and the crossing of several cold side creeks that descend from cirques high above the canyon. The summits above the canyon to the left average 12,600' and are unnamed.

At mile 4.4 the trail crosses Flint Creek and up until midsummer you usually have to wade through the stream. There are more side creeks and some steep climbing until you meet Rock Creek Trail (No. 11) at mile 7.0. Flint Lake (11,620') is nearby but hidden by trees and boulders.

NO. 18 – SIERRA VANDERA CREEK TRAIL (Manway)

Trailhead elevation   –   9,560'
Total vertical ascent   –   3,220'
Highest point   –   12,180'
Total vertical descent   –   2,900'
Length –   10.0 miles one way
Maps –   7½' Granite Lake
          7½' Emerald Lake
          7½' Granite Peak
          San Juan National Forest

If you are advanced in your backpacking techniques, possess equipment suitable for the conditions that exist above timberline and can use topographic maps for route-finding, you may consider Sierra Vandera Trail.* To be exact, this is actually the Pine-Piedra Stock Driveway which descends Sierra Vandera Creek and ends at the Pine River Trail (No. 14). I have listed a trailhead (0) on the Piedra Road (mile 38.5) but this is the most likely place for the trail to terminate. The trail description will begin at the other end,

---

*The Spanish meaning of Sierra Vandera is unsure, but probably "vandera" has come from the word "bandera" which means banner or flag; an appropriate name since Sierra Vandera Creek curves around Flag Mountain. Sierra, of course, means mountain or mountain range.

at the Pine River Trail. The reason is that most of the hikers on this trail will be people who wish an adventurous excursion away from the relatively well-known Pine River country. This old stock driveway, one of the routes by which herders brought sheep into the Pine River area has seen no use in recent years. The trail is not maintained by the Forest Service at present and is, for the purpose of this guidebook, a manway.

You begin the trail at mile 13.2 on the Pine River Trail (No. 14). The difficult crossing of the Pine at this point should not be attempted until after mid-summer when the waters have receded somewhat.   At any rate, this must be considered a dangerous crossing for backpackers. You should use a strong stick as a third leg, and be able to free yourself from your pack should the water throw you down. An alternative would be to take the Pine River Trail .5 mile further to where the valley levels out and the waters are less turbulent but deeper, cross to the east side of the river and return downstream to Sierra Vandera Trail. A 200' bench is climbed just after the river crossing; then the trail begins to climb steadily through aspen until at mile 1.4 it swings south. Here you cross, and probably wade, Sierra Vandera Creek. A little further on the possibility of an excellent campsite presents itself as the trail levels out. The canyon has broadened considerably and from this point you might pursue some interesting explorations of the benches leading southwest up to Flag Mountain (12,323'). Sierra Vandera Creek is crossed again at mile 1.9 and the trail begins to climb once more. Now the forest changes to spruce and fir, and Sierra Vandera Creek is not far away on your right. Finally at mile 4.0, after ascending 1,000' in the last 2.0 miles you reach the ridgetop between Bald Mountain (12,255') on your left (northeast) and Flag Mountain to the right. There is a trail going to the east (left) around Bald Mountain. You will keep right along the ridge with the old driveway as it climbs 200' and then descends to the head of Falls Creek at mile 5.25. The trail continues south, climbing now and finding the easiest way around the humps and hills along the ridge. At mile 6.25 after rounding a tree-covered knoll the U.S.G.S. map shows the trail turning left suddenly and descending. This is the Sand Creek Trail, which may be difficult to see, and it would take you to the Piedra Road. Sierra Vandera Trail (the old driveway) that stays with the ridge and now begins to rise toward Graham Peak will be hard to see at times and is criss-crossed by strong game trails at certain points. It is shown only on the Forest Service map and the guidebook map.

Crossing the saddle and going up the grassy flat-topped ridge you will find the trail down a few feet from the right side. After another saddle, turn left and traverse around a high hill. Soon (mile 7.0) you can see a very beautiful unnamed lake lying in the basin below you. This would be a good high altitude campsite. As you continue past the lake and reach another saddle you must keep right as the ridge rises steeply with a big drop-off to the Pine River valley (west). Left, across a small draw you may see another trail, but pay no attention to it as you reach a level bench. You can see the trail ahead contouring around the steep mountainside that drops away to Willow Park, 3,600' below. Another couple of benches and you continue keeping left and descend diagonally to find some crude switchbacks. The trail becomes very clear as you pass below the conspicuous "notch" of Graham Peak (mile 7.5). More contouring around a ridge and a little climbing and you are traveling at 12,120' below the summit of 12,531' Graham Peak. Climb the peak and be rewarded with one of the finest 360-degree views imaginable. The trail is now shown on the U.S.G.S. Granite Peak quadrangle. It then leaves the steep side of Graham Peak and finds the easiest way along a ridge that runs southwest. At mile 8.5 the trail plunges down through a steep gully to the left and then into thick forest for 1.5 miles to end at Piedra Road (No. 631) and trailhead (0) at mile 10.0. The trail is easy to lose in the forest when you descend because the faded yellow stock driveway markers attached to trees along the route are visible to the south, for someone ascending. Watch for blazed trees. Where you come out on the road there is only a little sign on a tree above the road identifying trail No. 1597 (Forest Service No.) to point out this little-used trail.

NO. 19 – DIVIDE LAKES TRAIL

Trailhead elevation   —   9,920'
Total vertical ascent   —   120'
Highest point   —   10,000'
Total vertical descent —   200'
Length   —   1.8 miles one way
Maps — 7½' Granite Lake
              San Juan National Forest

About .3 mile north of the Granite Peak Guard Station on the Pine River Trail (No. 14) you turn right at mile 15.8 to Divide Lakes Trail. The crossing of the Pine River here is not difficult after the run-off has slackened. Across the river you will find Granite Lake Trail (No. 20) going left on a bench above the river bottom. After a little climbing on your trail, you will be in the vicinity of three of the Divide Lakes, which are actually beaver dams. At .5 mile you arrive at the biggest Divide Lake (10,000'). With its light-colored shoreline and water reflecting the dark green trees, Divide Lake is enchanting. Old maps show two lakes here but the beavers have engineered a controlled outlet and raised the water level to form one lake. You can see trees around the perimeter that were drowned when this happened. Late or early in the day you may see beaver cruising the lake. There are some windy campsites around the north and west sides of big Divide Lake. In all lakes of the Divide group fishing is good.

The trail continues around the north side of the lake and at mile 1.0 you begin a descent of 200' to Weminuche Creek at mile 1.4. Don't confuse this with the Weminuche Creek on the Rio Grande side. At mile 1.8 you meet the Piedra Stock Driveway (No. 23).

NO. 20 — GRANITE LAKE TRAIL

Trailhead elevation   —   9,920'
Total vertical ascent —   400'
Highest point   --   10,320'
Length   —   1.0 mile one way
Maps — 7½' Granite Lake
        San Juan National Forest

You find Granite Lake Trail going left from Divide Lakes Trail (No. 19) just after it has crossed the Pine River. The trail proceeds north on benches above the river flats and at .5 mile climbs 400' to big (32-acre) cobalt blue Granite Lake (10,310'). The steep sides of granite which are aspen-covered on the north shoreline and spruce-covered on the south shoreline plunge into the lake which appears to be very deep. This trail does not connect with the Piedra Driveway which has a 1.5 mile cut-off that passes the east side of the lake. There is space for one or two small

Divide Lake

parties to camp. The fishing is variable, but big fish have been caught here.

NO. 21 — SNOWSLIDE CANYON TRAIL

Trailhead elevation   —   10,240'
Total vertical ascent —   1,720'
Highest point   —   11,960'
Length —   4.0 miles one way
Maps — 7½' Weminuche Pass
        San Juan National Forest

The trail up Snowslide Canyon is not on the U.S.G.S. quadrangle. Snowslide Canyon may have sheep grazing although the author has not experienced this.

Snowslide Canyon Trail is found in the Pine River Valley in a secluded meadow at the mouth of Snowslide Canyon. Snowslide Creek turns abruptly north on the edge of the meadow and the trail crosses about 50 yards before the turn. This meadow can be reached by turning right and crossing the Pine at mile 18.25 on the Pine River Trail (No. 14). In .5 mile east you climb up to the mouth of Snowslide Canyon. Also at mile 19.0 on the Pine River Trail, just before La Osa Creek, the Piedra Stock Driveway (No. 23) is met coming from the southeast across the Pine River and Snowslide Creek and you can follow this trail back .75 mile to the meadows where Snowslide Trail begins. If the Pine River looks too big to cross, go over La Osa Creek first and then ford the much-reduced Pine above the mouth of La Osa.

The 1,700' of climb on the trail is distributed fairly evenly throughout the 4.0 miles of ascent to the Continental Divide and the Continental Divide Trail (No. 59). The trail stays on the north side of the creek and initially passes through aspen and enticing meadows. Since this trail is not used by many people your chances of encountering some wildlife are good. You might surprise a small band of elk grazing at the edge of a meadow as you climb up this trail. The many snowslide paths denuded of foliage are easy to see in the first 1.0 mile or so.

At mile 2.0 the trail climbs through spruce and fir away from what looks like the main canyon. Soon however, you break into meadows and approach the Continental Divide at the head of

Snowslide Canyon, broad and gently rolling country. The trail soon becomes faint and you will have to keep a sharp eye for the occasional post-markers that show the way. The trail does not go over to the lowest point on the Divide but keeps left and climbs a low ridge to meet the Continental Divide Trail (No. 59) at mile 4.0 where that trail is just about to go into the North Fork of the Pine canyon.

NO. 22 — RINCON LA OSA TRAIL

Trailhead elevation   —   10,162'
Total vertical ascent —   2,078'
Highest point   —   12,240'
Length — 6.0 miles one way
Maps — 7½' Weminuche Pass
      7½' Rio Grande Pyramid
      San Juan National Forest

Rincon La Osa* Trail is well known by outfitters who frequent the Pine and Vallecito country. Throughout the summer, dudes are packed into either the meadows at La Osa Creek's mouth or the open country around the last 3.0 miles of the trail. Later, the outfitter returns to pick them up at a specified date. La Osa Trail is not in good shape and the many bogs and springs along the trail make it difficult for foot travel after the heavy horse traffic.

The trail begins at mile 19.0 of the Pine River Trail (No. 14). As you proceed up the trail through the meadow you may cross La Osa Creek wherever it looks easiest. Walking along the right side of the creek you will find the well worn trail where the dense forest begins. As you continue up the trail you will notice many places where the Forest Service has constructed elaborate ramps of logs in order to make a good tread through the wettest spots. Looking down the trail you should have some good views of the Pine River Valley and into Snowslide Canyon on the east side. After some steep climbing you break into meadows at mile 2.0. The meadows of upper La Osa are particularly beautiful with the pink granite outcrops here and there and dark heavy forest on

---

*Rincon, as it is used in the southwest mountains, often refers to a little valley, frequently with meadows. La Osa means the bear, in Spanish.

either side of the Rincon. As you cross La Osa Creek (mile 3.8) you are in the broad expanse of meadows that form the lower reaches of a basin rimmed by mountains which are capped by light-colored volcanics. If you follow the stream through the thick grass of the meadow for a little ways you will find that it has a narrow channel with undercut banks that are the hiding places for large numbers of trout. The trail continues for another 1.0 mile and then you begin the final steep ascent to the Continental Divide Trail (No. 59) at mile 6.0.

III.

The Volcanic Mountains

	trailhead	length
No. 23 — Piedra Stock Driveway (Weminuche Creek)	(K)	10.5 miles
No. 24 — East Fork of Weminuche Creek Trail		4.75 miles
No. 25 — Hossick Creek Trail		7.6 miles
No. 26 — Hossick Lake Trail		.6 mile
No. 27 — Cimarrona Creek Trail	(L)	6.5 miles
No. 28 — Williams Creek Trail	(M)	9.5 miles
No. 29 — Williams Lake Trail		2.25 miles
No. 30 — Indian Creek Trail		8.25 miles
No. 31 — Palisade Meadows Cut-off		2.0 miles
No. 32 — Indian Creek Cut-off		1.3 miles
No. 33 — Middle Fork Trail	(N)	10.6 miles
No. 34 — Deadman Creek Trail (Manway)		2.25 miles
No. 35 — Fourmile Creek Trail	(P)	7.0 miles
No. 36 — Fourmile Lake Trail		1.0 mile
No. 37 — Turkey Creek Trail	(Q)	18.6 miles
No. 38 — West Fork Trail	(R)	11.75 miles
No. 39 — Beaver Creek Trail		9.5 miles
		113.95 miles

The volcanic mountains rise abruptly from the surrounding country with 2,000' (on the average) volcanic cliffs and summits around 12,500' and are a sharp contrast to the Needles and granitic mountains further west. Thick volcanic twisted and contorted deposits give the area a wild look not found anywhere else in the Weminuche Wilderness. The Continental Divide winds its way east through this section with many of the trails ascending through dark rough canyons cut into the volcanic layers.

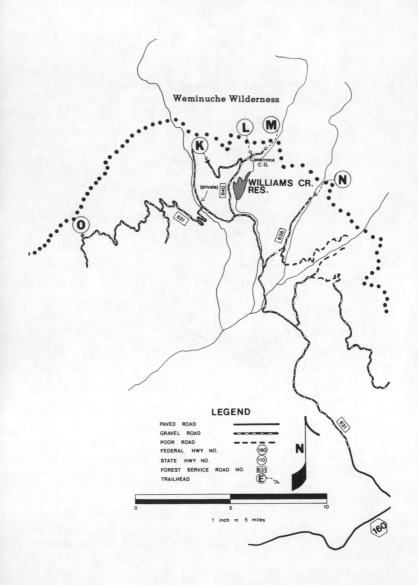

Weminuche Wilderness

K L M

Cimarrona
C.G.

WILLIAMS CR.
RES.

(private) 640

631

536

N

O

LEGEND

PAVED ROAD	————————
GRAVEL ROAD	— — — —
POOR ROAD	– – – –
FEDERAL HWY NO.	160
STATE HWY NO.	110
FOREST SERVICE ROAD NO.	631
TRAILHEAD	E

N

631

160

0   5   10

1 inch = 5 miles

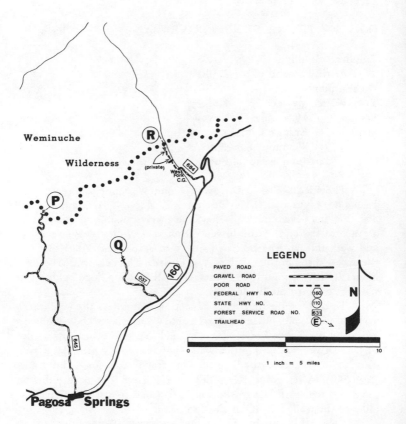

LEGEND

PAVED ROAD	
GRAVEL ROAD	
POOR ROAD	
FEDERAL HWY NO.	160
STATE HWY NO.	110
FOREST SERVICE ROAD NO.	631
TRAILHEAD	E

N

0   5   10

1 inch = 5 miles

Weminuche

Wilderness

P

Q

R

(private)

West Fork C.G.

664

037

160

645

Pagosa Springs

There is probably no trail in these mountains which is as heavily used as in the Needle Mountains and the Vallecito and Pine River country. But the potential for many exciting backpack trips is overwhelming. Trails No. 28, No. 35 and No. 36, and No. 37 (to mile 9.0) have moderate numbers of fishermen. The access is generally good for all trails.

NO. 23 — PIEDRA STOCK DRIVEWAY — — — (Trailhead K)

Trailhead elevation   —   9,120'
Total vertical ascent   —   2,400'
Highest point   —   10,880'
Total vertical descent —   1,558'
Length   —   10.5 miles one way
Maps —   7½' Granite Lake
            7½' Weminuche Pass
            San Juan National Forest

The Piedra Stock Driveway along Weminuche Creek (San Juan side) takes you to Divide Lakes Trail (No. 19), Granite Lake, and the Pine River country. It was formerly possible to drive up to a ranch at the end of the lower Weminuche Valley, leave your car and walk through the ranch property to reach the trail. However, the access through the ranch is now closed. The new route requires hikers to drive to another point and walk down a ridge behind the ranch to get into the Wilderness.

To find the Piedra Driveway section that enters the Wilderness you go about 3.0 miles west of Pagosa Springs on U.S. Highway 160 until the Forest Service Piedra Road (No. 631) turns off to the right. Drive for 22.0 miles (the first few miles paved) on this usually good gravel road until you reach Williams Lake Road (No. 640). After going 3.5 miles up this road and past Williams Lake you will turn left on Poison Park Road (No. 644). Drive 3.0 miles to the trailhead (K) at the end of the road.

The trail begins by descending a steep 640' ridge in the first 1.5 miles to enter the Weminuche Valley. It skirts the ranch fences until mile 2.1, when you come to the corner of the fenced private land. Hossick Creek Trail (No. 25) may be seen on your right at this corner but you should follow the fence about 100 yards or less after the corner. After you cross an irrigation ditch you can find the trail going immediately to the right. At mile 2.4 you cross Hossick Creek which can be rough in early summer, especially if there is a lot of run-off. Soon the trail comes to a large meadow, where you must look for the post-markers that guide you to the middle of the meadow where the trail goes on clearly. The view up to the rough volcanic layered cliffs over 3,000' high is excellent. At mile 3.0 you cross the aptly named Milk Creek. The trail begins to climb and soon enters a narrow canyon. At mile 4.0 just after crossing the canyon's small stream you must keep right and climb gradually along the hiking trail instead of the steep climb straight ahead on the stock driveway. The trails meet in the level area above. On the edge of the bench is a view of the valley below which can satisfy you for hours. Be sure to notice the beautiful milky quartz outcrop that comprises the knob on which you are sitting.

The trail is distinct as you cross several streams and walk through the wide Weminuche Creek valley. Ahead and to the left, high on the valley wall you can see some waterfalls that descend great distances as silver threads. This is excellent elk country and I have often surprised small herds in the aspen and meadows through which the trail passes. The timber changes to spruce as the trail approaches the mouth of the canyon of Weminuche Creek's East Fork which you cross at mile 6.5 on a bridge. A few feet into the meadow beyond the crossing you will see the East Fork of the Weminuche Trail (No. 24) going right. Here at the East Fork is good camping, although the presence of several messy hunter's camps is not appreciated. Continuing through mixed aspen and conifer forest at mile 7.25, you find Divide Lake Trail (No. 19) taking off left. Your trail soon brings you close to Weminuche Creek, then crosses and climbs steeply up the point of a ridge. When you reach a bench (mile 8.0) the trail divides and you have the choice of going left to visit the east side of Granite Lake, then climb out of Granite Lake's pocket and rejoin the main trail; or simply climbing ahead and traversing the fairly level but somewhat boggy country above Granite Lake. Around mile 9.0 the trail begins to descend into the Pine River valley. At mile 10.0 you pass the meadows at the mouth of Snowslide Canyon and Snowslide Creek Trail (No. 21). Proceed on, cross Snowslide Creek and then the Pine River to meet the Pine River Trail (No. 14) at mile 10.5.

NO. 24 – EAST FORK OF WEMINUCHE CREEK TRAIL

Trailhead elevation   –   9,520'
Total vertical ascent –   1,680'
Highest point   –   11,200'
Length   –   4.75 miles one way
Maps – 7½' Granite Lake
          San Juan National Forest

This trail is found at mile 6.5 on the Piedra Stock Driveway (No. 23) just after crossing the East Fork on a bridge. The trail goes right through the meadow that follows, and climbs 4.75 miles to a magnificent cul-de-sac under the Continental Divide. The East Fork of the Weminuche is a big creek and some fine fishing can be found upstream on this tumbling beauty. There are few signs of man's intrusion.

Close to where the trail crosses the good-sized creek coming down from Grouse Rincon (mile 1.75), a camp can be set up and used as a point from which you can explore and discover this wild canyon for yourself. Once the canyon has curved to the right the Continental Divide is at the top of the north canyon walls, 2,400' above you. Storms seem particularly intense over this rugged and deeply incised canyon. You will notice the obvious paths of numerous snowslides spanning the distance from top to bottom. The avalanches are a good example of the mass wasting brought on by the continuous tug of gravity exerting itself on these steep slopes.

NO. 25 – HOSSICK CREEK TRAIL

Trailhead elevation   –   8,480'
Total vertical ascent –   4,040'
Highest point   –   12,320'
Total vertical descent –   1,320'
Length   –   7.6 miles one way
Maps – 7½' Granite Lake
          7½' Cimarrona Peak
          San Juan National Forest

Hossick Creek Trail begins at mile 2.1 on the Piedra Stock

Squaw Pass

Driveway (No. 23) at the corner of fenced private land. There is no sign or marker but you will see it angling away from the corner as it heads toward Hossick Creek which it soon crosses. In years with heavy run-off Hossick Creek is high and rolling, and it is difficult to cross until mid-summer. Until Hossick Creek is crossed again at mile 1.75, the trail works its way up a narrow gorge at approximately a 15% grade with noisy Hossick Creek close by. From the second crossing, the way is still steep although there are sections where the climbing moderates from time to time. The forest cover is continually dense. At mile 3.5 you begin leaving the timber behind as the trail levels out into the large basin at the head of Hossick Creek, nestled into Cimarrona Peak (12,536') and the Continental Divide. The basin offers the first good camping up to this point on the trail. Hossick Lake lies above and behind the steep cliffs on the left and around the basin to the right, volcanic cliffs end in a spectacular jutting point (12,577') that was known as Cimarrona Peak. When the new U.S.G.S. 7½' quadrangle was completed, a summit 1.0 mile north was assigned that name.

The trail climbs out of the basin curving left as it begins to ascend the steep headwall. It meets Hossick Lake Trail (No. 26) at mile 4.1, then swings right to pass just below the summit of 12,536' Cimarrona Peak at mile 4.75. The peak is an easy climb of only a little over 200' to the top and the view is great. The trail crosses over to the Cimarrona Creek drainage past a jagged, volcanic knife-edge pass and descends to a small basin. Below this basin Cimarrona Creek Trail is met at mile 5.5 directly at timberline. After meeting Cimarrona Creek Trail,* Hossick Creek Trail turns suddenly left, contours around and finally climbs to attain a ridge extending out from Cimarrona Peak. From this point, the trail loses 600' in elevation as it descends to the open and rolling glaciated divide that is Squaw Pass (11,200') at mile 7.6. At Squaw Pass the Continental Divide Trail (No. 59) and Squaw Creek Trail (No. 51) are found.

The amount of vertical ascent and descent on Hossick Creek Trail make it one of the more challenging hikes but also very rewarding scenically.

---

*Cimarrona Creek Trail (No. 27), a shorter way to reach the same country (Squaw Pass and the Continental Divide), is a carefully constructed switchbacked trail, beginning from trailhead (L).

NO. 26 — HOSSICK LAKE TRAIL

Trailhead elevation   —   11,800'
Total vertical ascent   —   280'
Highest point   —   12,080'
Total vertical descent —   200'
Length   —   .6 mile one way
Maps — 7½' Cimarrona Peak
        San Juan National Forest

The .6 mile trail for Hossick Lake leaves Hossick Creek Trail (No. 25) at mile 4.1 where it has climbed part way up the steep headwall of its basin. The trail to Hossick Lake goes left and climbs 280' over some very precipitous cliffs that are in front of the cirque basin in which Hossick Lake (11,886') is located. This rocky basin with wild peaks around it has no camping right by the lake; instead you will have to climb a little higher above the lake to find an area that is level enough and has sufficient earth to pitch a tent. Make sure your equipment is suitable for the more severe conditions at high altitude which include no wood for warmth and cooking. The unnamed summits around the basin are: west, 12,760'; north, 12,967'; and east, 12,630'.

NO. 27 — CIMARRONA CREEK TRAIL — — — (Trailhead L)

Trailhead elevation   —   8,400'
Total vertical ascent   —   3,200'
Highest point   —   11,600'
Length   —   6.5 miles one way
Maps — 7½' Cimarrona Peak
        San Juan National Forest

The trailhead (L) for Cimarrona Creek Trail is on the left side of the road just beyond the entrance to Cimarrona Campground. To reach Cimarrona Campground you take Forest Service Piedra Road (No. 631) as described in trail No. 23 to Williams Lake Road (No. 640). Cimarrona Creek Trail begins on Williams Lake Road at mile 4.1.

The new Forest Service Cimarrona Trail is shown only on the guidebook's map. It was finished in the summer of 1975 and

replaces the dangerous manway that ascended the east side of the
creek and which appears on the U.S.G.S. quadrangle. The new trail,
although well laid out, climbs 3,200' in 6.5 miles to ascend the
volcanic cliffs characteristic of this part of the wilderness, and no
possibilities of camping exist until around mile 5.75.

The trail wanders from side to side of a low ridge, through
conifers and aspen with an army of gray squirrels that scold you
unforgivingly at every step. The forest cover is dense and at mile
2.0 the trail begins to switchback and climb in earnest. As you
gain altitude you begin to have some views of Williams Lake and the
hills that roll away to the south. The many well-planned switchbacks take you up past the volcanic cliffs with unusual shapes and
colors. At one point the trail goes through a natural arch of
volcanic rock. (My guess is that this was probably a lava tube
which was somehow cut off just back of its opening, leaving an
arch).

The trail finally levels out to contour around a ridge with
some pretty waterfalls spraying down to the trail. At mile 5.75 the
trail suddenly turns left, where the old trail is met, to climb steeply
up and around a small basin, and at mile 6.5 it meets Hossick Creek
Trail (No. 25).

From here you can take Hossick Creek Trail straight on, then
right to find the Continental Divide Trail (No. 59) in a little over
2.0 miles at Squaw Pass (11,200'). Or you can go left on Hossick
Creek Trail as it climbs over the steep ridge into Hossick Creek, and
visit Hossick Lake (11,886'), again a little over 2.0 miles distant.

NO. 28 — WILLIAMS CREEK TRAIL — — — (Trailhead M)

Trailhead elevation   —   8,360'
Total vertical ascent —   3,540'
Highest point   —   11,900'
Length —   9.5 miles one way
Maps — 7½' Cimarrona Peak
       7½' Little Squaw Creek
       San Juan National Forest

Locate Williams Lake Road as described in Trail No. 23. The
trailhead (M) for Williams Creek Trail is at the end of Williams
Lake Road (No. 640), mile 4.75.

From the trail sign you walk for .25 mile on the road through an unimproved campground. The trail begins and soon climbs to a pleasant bench that has a fair number of Ponderosa pine in addition to the usual aspen and Douglas fir found at this elevation. Here, and especially around the Ponderosas, you might get a glimpse of the somewhat rare tassel-eared squirrel (also known as Abert squirrel). With their distinctive tufted ears and large silvery tail they are one of the most beautiful small mammals you will ever see.

The old Spanish name for Williams Creek was Huerto: garden-like. The first few miles of Williams Creek do give the impression of a gigantic, walled garden. Across the creek to the right, a group of peaks eroded from the volcanic rock and cliffs with waterfalls conjure up images of a South Pacific island. After passing a couple of creeks that tumble over volcanic rock stream-beds you reach a meadow at mile 2.4. Indian Creek Trail (No. 30) leaves your trail at this point to make a crossing of Williams Creek. A little further on, at mile 3.1 you will have to cross Williams Creek and if it is still early in the summer the creek could give you a hard time. After this crossing the trail begins climbing and at mile 4.5 you look left up the trailless and steep-walled canyon that ends at Squaw Pass. The trail curves right with the main canyon and Williams Creek (now smaller) is crossed once more (mile 6.5). At mile 7.4 you meet the 2.25-mile Williams Lake Trail (No. 29) that would take you to the Continental Divide Trail (No. 59), Williams and Trout Lakes and the Trout Creek Trail (No. 47). You keep left and climb hard for a little more than 2.0 miles to meet the Continental Divide Trail (No. 59) at mile 9.5. The view down into Little Squaw Creek from the Continental Divide is one you won't forget soon.

NO. 29 — WILLIAMS LAKE TRAIL

Trailhead elevation   —   10,660'
Total vertical ascent —   1,340'
Highest point   —   12,000'
Length   —   2.25 miles one way
Maps — 7½' Cimarrona Peak
         7½' Little Squaw Creek
         San Juan National Forest

    This steep trail leaves Williams Creek Trail (No. 28) at mile
7.4 to climb to Williams Lake (11,695') at mile 1.75 and meet the
Continental Divide Trail (No. 59) at mile 2.25. The lake is above
timberline, so conditions for camping can be severe.

    The larger, but man-raised Trout Lake lies in a similar basin
1.0 mile across the Continental Divide. It appears that two glaciers
ground away at their headwalls and nearly leveled them to create
the almost valley-like rolling divide you see between Williams and
Trout Lakes. Texas Creek Trail (No. 50) and Trout Creek Trail
(No. 47) are found near Trout Lake.

NO. 30 — INDIAN CREEK TRAIL

Trailhead elevation   —   9,000'
Total vertical ascent —   3,640'
Highest point   —   11,640'
Total vertical descent —   1,000'
Length   —   8.25 miles one way
Maps — 7½' Cimarrona Peak
         7½' Palomino Mountain
         San Juan National Forest

    The Indian Creek Trail is one of the most interesting in the
volcanic mountains of the Wilderness. It ends at the Continental
Divide Trail (No. 59) and there are two trails passed enroute,
Palisade Meadows Cut-off (No. 31) and Indian Creek Cut-off
(No. 32), that ascend to the Divide as well. Where Indian Creek
Trail and Indian Creek Cut-off reach the Divide there are no signs
or markers which makes these trails hard to locate from the Con-
tinental Divide Trail.

Indian Creek Trail leaves Williams Creek Trail (No. 28) at mile 2.4. Williams Creek is crossed and, through mid-summer, most likely forded without shoes and socks. The trail continues by climbing up the deeply incised canyon of Indian Creek. The volcanic layers high above the creek look as if they have just come to rest and cooled. At mile 2.2 you cross Indian Creek briefly for five switchbacks and then return to the left side. Both crossings might require wading. The canyon has narrowed to a cleft in the plateau ahead through which the trail climbs. Once more it crosses Indian Creek just as it levels out into the expansive Palisade Meadows (10,800'). You can find a number of good places to camp around the edges of these meadows. Campsites in Palisade Meadows are more than likely to be visited by a pair of inquisitive gray jays, called "camp robbers". At mile 3.5, just after crossing Indian Creek once more, the 2.0-mile Palisade Meadows Cut-off goes left in the timber to the Continental Divide.

Leaving Palisade Meadows our trail climbs over a ridge to enter Pistol Park (11,000'), a sloping meadow full of miner's candles. The U.S.G.S. topographic map is inaccurate about the trail in Palisade Meadows and here, as you descend to the Middle Fork of the Piedra River, where eleven switchbacks are not shown. Looking down the Middle Fork of the Piedra, one can easily understand why the Spanish gave it the name Alboroto Creek: disturbed and agitated. As the trail begins ascending along the left side of the Middle Fork there are some particularly nice angled bedrock troughs up to 50 yards long through which the river shoots. At mile 6.25 the canyon changes drastically from the wild disorder to a spacious open park set in rounded mountains that lead to the Continental Divide. This park and surrounding mountains could be explored for many days from a camp at this location*. Some years, however, this is used as a camp for a sheep outfit. The trail crosses the river at mile 6.7 and straight ahead at the edge of the timber Indian Creek Cut-off (No. 32) can be found. About 100 yards after crossing, you cross a stream on the right and keep right of another creek. The blazed tree at the edge of the

---

*A disreputable mule-packer "highgraded" gold ore from Beartown and, after making a getaway along the Continental Divide, cached his riches in the vicinity of the meadow at the head of the Middle Fork. Read Sheepherder's Gold by Temple Cornelius, Sage Books, for details.

meadow shows where the trail continues. The rest of the way is a steep climb to the Continental Divide Trail (No. 59) at mile 8.25, elevation 11,040'. If you want to find this trail from the Continental Divide there are no cairns or signs; you will have to read the topographic map to locate the correct saddle and begin finding the trail as you descend from that point.

NO. 31 – PALISADE MEADOWS CUT-OFF

Trailhead elevation   —   10,880'
Total vertical ascent —   1,070'
Highest point   —   11,950'
Length — 2.0 miles one way
Maps — 7½' Cimarrona Peak
        San Juan National Forest

The Palisade Meadows Cut-off is found at mile 3.5 on Indian Creek Trail (No. 30) and climbs through dense forest to reach the Continental Divide Trail (No. 59) in 2.0 miles. In Palisade Meadows, Indian Creek Trail has just crossed to the north side of the creek and a small sign saying: Continental Divide — 2 miles, indicates the beginning of the cut-off. At the other end, on the Divide Trail, there is a cairn to mark the location of the cut-off which begins where the south-going Continental Divide Trail suddenly swings east.

NO. 32 – INDIAN CREEK CUT-OFF

Trailhead elevation   —   10,520'
Total vertical ascent —   1,040'
Highest point   —   11,560'
Length — 1.3 miles one way
Maps — 7½' Palomino Mountain
        San Juan National Forest

The Indian Creek Cut-off begins in the meadow at the head of the Middle Fork of the Piedra River. Indian Creek Trail (No. 30) has just crossed the Piedra River (mile 6.7), then turns and crosses a stream on the right. Instead of crossing the second stream you must walk straight ahead to the edge of the timber and locate the blazed trees. Indian Creek Cut-off climbs in 1.3 miles to the Continental Divide Trail (No. 59), elevation 11,560'.

As with the end of Indian Creek Trail there are no signs or markers at the Divide Trail. To begin Indian Creek Cut-off from the Continental Divide, you will have to read the topographic map to deduce from which saddle the trail begins, determine your own position, and then pick up the trail as you begin to descend.

NO. 33 — MIDDLE FORK TRAIL — — — (Trailhead N)

Trailhead elevation   —   8,400'
Total vertical ascent   —   4,600'
Highest point   —   12,160'
Total vertical descent   —   1,040'
Length   —   10.6 miles one way
Maps — 7½' Cimarrona Peak
        7½' Palomino Mountain
        San Juan National Forest

To reach the trailhead (N) for the Middle Fork Trail you drive on Forest Service Piedra Road (No. 631) as described in Trail No. 23 to a junction at mile 17.8. Here you go right on Toner Road (No. 636). This road goes past Chub Draw Road (left) and a road (right) that would take you to the East Fork of the Piedra River. The road ends when you reach the Middle Fork Hunter Campground at mile 23.3 with the last couple of miles becoming somewhat rough. The steep volcanic cliffs rise abruptly around the meadow where the trail begins, and Toner Mountain (12,495') is over 4,000' above you to the east.

The trail goes right from the road to cross the Middle Fork of the Piedra River (Piedra: Spanish for rock). This will be a difficult if not impossible crossing until the spring run-off has slowed. The last half of the trail stays close to, or over 12,000', so if the Middle Fork of the Piedra is still a difficult crossing there is probably too much snow on the high part of the trail anyway. At mile .8 the trail begins the steep climb up Lean Creek's canyon. Finally, after passing just left of Sugarloaf Mountain (12,593'), the trail reaches an elevation of about 12,160' at mile 5.3. Your reward for ascending a 15% grade (on the average) over the last 4.5 miles is an unsurpassed view from a high ridge into the heart of the volcanic mountains that are found in this section of the Wilderness. This is the kind of country where you might get a good look at a golden eagle riding the air currents near the peaks. The trail continues by finding the easiest way along the top of this rough SW — NE ridge between Porphyry Gulch on the left and East Fork of the Piedra River on the right.

From mile 5.3 the trail descends, then climbs to round a 12,338' summit. It passes through a saddle (the window) above Window Lake (11,600'). This would be a possible campsite although there is more level ground and room at Monument Lake, still ahead. The trail contours around Window Lake's basin, crosses to the left of the ridgeline, and rounds a 12,017' summit. Once more, it crosses a saddle to a basin on the east side of the ridge. Here at mile 7.25, with difficulty you can find Deadman Creek Manway (No. 34) where it begins its descent to the East Fork of the Piedra River. The trail proceeds around a 12,247' summit on the east and arrives at Monument Lake (11,600') at mile 8.0. Although Monument Lake is not the prettiest lake in the Weminuche Wilderness, it will probably be a pleasant change from the circuitous route just completed. A good stand of spruce to the west helps lessen the usual windiness of passes and saddles. The trail crosses the stream from the lake and you must locate a sign on one of the trees north of the lake that says: Continental Divide — 1 mile. As you leave the lake through the dense timber there are some bad blowdowns over the trail. You persist, and soon the trail climbs right around a 12,330' summit and reaches Palomino Mountain (12,230') and the Continental Divide at mile 9.0. The obvious trail and the one shown on the U.S.G.S. topographic map contours left around Palomino Mountain and some other palomino-colored summits to meet the Continental Divide Trail (No. 59) at mile 10.6. You can also climb over Palomino Mountain and meet the Divide Trail in .5 mile on the other side. There will also be a faint trail going right. This manway leads to a small valley just below the Continental Divide which you can follow down to the East Fork of the Piedra River to meet Turkey Creek Trail (No. 37).

The Middle Fork Trail is steep, exposed to storms and offers little camping. For someone who likes the howl of wind across the rocks and high peaks, the challenge of this trail is very enticing.

NO. 34 – DEADMAN CREEK TRAIL – (Manway)

Trailhead elevation   –   11,760'
Total vertical descent –   2,280'
Highest point   –   11,760'
Length   –   2.25 miles one way
Maps – 7½' Palomino Mountain
        San Juan National Forest

Deadman Creek Manway is shown on the guidebook's map, the Forest Service map, and partially on the U.S.G.S. quadrangle. This manway is recommended only for persons advanced in back-packing and route-finding skills.

The trail begins its descent into the East Fork of the Piedra River at mile 7.25 of the Middle Fork Trail (No. 33). The Middle Fork Trail has just crossed a saddle to the east side of the ridge and contours around a small basin. Just after entering this basin, at mile 7.25, drop down from the Middle Fork Trail keeping right of a small stream and locate blazes on the trees that will get you started on the Deadman Manway. When the basin begins to slope away steeply toward the river valley the path becomes fairly clear. It is criss-crossed by strong game trails, however, so you must always keep a sharp eye out for blazed trees.

After 2.25 miles of walking around blown-down timber and past several small streams, the trail drops off an aspen-covered bench and crosses a small creek close to the Piedra River. Shortly thereafter it crosses the river to arrive in the vicinity of Deadman Creek. The bottom of the canyon is a wild and exciting place, with a few small campsites to be found here and there. The fishing is good, exploring is limitless, and there will probably be no one around to bother you. Upon crossing Deadman Creek you can make out bits of a trail that will take you to some meadows .25 mile up a small side canyon close to the mouth of Deadman Creek where good camping can be found. The Forest Service map shows a trail continuing on up Deadman Creek from this point, but so far I have found only game trails and tough going on this route.

NO. 35 — FOURMILE CREEK TRAIL — — — (Trailhead P)

Trailhead elevation   —   9,200'
Total vertical ascent   —   3,080'
Highest point   —   11,920'
Total vertical descent —   1,000'
Length —   7.0 miles one way
Maps — 7½' Pagosa Peak
        San Juan National Forest

Fourmile Creek Trail has as its destination either Fourmile Lake (Fourmile Lake Trail No. 36) or Turkey Creek Lake and Turkey Creek Trail (No. 37). Because these lakes are an attraction to fishermen, Fourmile Trail receives more use than others in the vicinity. These lakes are not likely to be free of ice until the 4th of July in a normal year. The three fordings of Fourmile Creek would be difficult until after this time as well.

Fourmile Creek Trail is an old stock driveway. To reach the section that enters the Wilderness drive north on Fourmile Road (No. 645) from Highway 160 in Pagosa Springs. After 9.0 miles, reach a junction and keep right for 5.0 more miles on No. 645 to arrive at the Fourmile Creek trailhead (P).

After crossing a small stream the trail descends to the valley floor (mile .5) and winds through pleasant meadows along the west side of Fourmile Creek. The very rough-looking Eagle Mountain (12,007') is above the valley on the right. The forest cover becomes dense until the trail comes to an area beneath precipitous cliffs which have been the scene of many snowslides. At mile 2.8 the trail crosses a stream with a waterfall directly above. The waterfall breaks into millions of droplets as it showers down from a height of about 300'. After some hard climbing past the unusual and distorted volcanic rocks that characterize this section of the Wilderness, the big, thundering waterfall on Fourmile Creek is immediately on your right. Also, turn and look south down the U-shaped valley of Fourmile Creek laid out before you.

The valley narrows to a gorge after the big waterfall and the trail climbs steadily to an old dilapidated stock bridge at mile 3.4. The trail is badly eroded from years of stock use and crosses Fourmile Creek three times before meeting Fourmile Lake Trail (No. 36) at mile 4.25. These fordings of Fourmile Creek will be difficult up until mid-summer. The trail climbs a steep gulch around Cherry Cairn (12,511') to cross a pass (11,920') into Turkey Creek drainage amid many high, unnamed summits. From this point you descend 800' to the 11,135' Turkey Creek Lake at mile 6.5. The trail crosses the creek at the outlet of the lake and climbs up a steep hillside to meet Turkey Creek Trail (No. 37) at mile 7.0.

There is some camping around Turkey Creek Lake but if your equipment is capable of weathering storms above timberline there is some interesting camping below the pass where there are a number of small lakes. The U.S.G.S. quadrangle shows several trails between Fourmile and Turkey Lakes, either through Deadman Creek or north of Cherry Cairn. These trails, however, are only manways. The trail into Deadman Creek is really difficult and will provide more than enough entertainment for people who wish to leave the well-worn paths.

NO. 36 — FOURMILE LAKE TRAIL

Trailhead elevation   —   10,760'
Total vertical ascent —   425'
Highest point   —   11,185'
Length —   1.0 mile one way
Maps — 7½' Pagosa Peak
       San Juan National Forest

At mile 4.25 on Fourmile Creek Trail (No. 35), Fourmile Lake Trail goes left to climb 425' with several steep sections in 1.0 mile to 11,185' Fourmile Lake.

After departing from Fourmile Creek Trail, Fourmile Lake Trail soon enters a large meadow below imposing Cherry Cairn (12,511') on the right. These meadows below the reddish-colored mountain are more suitable for camping than the rather limited space around Fourmile Lake.

There are several trails around Fourmile Lake shown on the U.S.G.S. quadrangle which are, in fact, only manways. One climbs through the thick forest east of Fourmile Lake to pass north of Cherry Cairn and connect with Fourmile Creek Trail 1.0 mile before Turkey Creek Lake. Another manway leaves Fourmile Lake Trail in the meadows below Fourmile Lake and ascends the left side of a small creek entering the upper end of the meadow from the west. This difficult manway would be the most practical way to visit upper Fourmile Lake (11,640'). The map shows this manway continuing on into Deadman Creek and then climbing again into Turkey Creek Lake's basin. A visit to Deadman Creek is not for those who have difficulty in route-finding because the trail is very faint and the terrain uncompromising.

NO. 37 — TURKEY CREEK TRAIL — — — (Trailhead Q)

Trailhead elevation   —   8,240'
Total vertical ascent   —   5,080'
Highest point   —   12,200'
Total vertical descent —   1,960'
Length   —   18.6 miles one way
Maps — 15' Wolf Creek Pass
            7½' Pagosa Peak
            7½' Palomino Mountain
            San Juan National Forest

Turkey Creek Trail is the longest trail in this section of the Wilderness. It passes Turkey Creek Lake, Fourmile Creek Trail (No. 35), and ends at the Continental Divide Trail (No. 59) after 18.6 miles of some of the best scenery to be found in the entire Wilderness. From Turkey Creek Lake to the Continental Divide the trail receives little or no maintenance. Turkey Creek Trail and the West Fork Trail (No. 38) taken together as a circle are referred to as the Rainbow Trail by the Forest Service.

Go northeast from Pagosa Springs on Highway 160 toward Wolf Creek Pass for 7.3 miles until you find Jackson Mountain Road (No. 037) going left. Follow this good gravel road for 4.0 miles to the end where the trailhead (Q) for Turkey Creek Trail is located. This new trailhead for Turkey Creek Trail avoids the long and rough Snowball Road from Pagosa Springs.

After beginning, the trail is soon close enough to Turkey Creek for you to hear it on your right. The old trail is met where it crosses Turkey Creek to eventually end at Highway 160 but you must continue ahead until at about mile 1.0 where an irrigation ditch is crossed. The Snowball junction is reached a little further on. After going right at this junction with an old jeep road that now serves as a trail, you walk through foothills covered with mixed conifer and aspen. With exception of occasional views of Saddle Mountain (12,033') ahead and on the right the forest cover is dense and unrewarding scenically. Cows often graze along the creekside. After crossing a few creeks the semblance of a jeep road is gone. At mile 4.25 a fallen tree over a small creek can steer you off on a trail that crosses Turkey Creek to a hunter's camp. However you must continue on the left of Turkey Creek for a little over 1.0 mile more to where the canyon walls get narrow and rise abruptly. Turkey Creek is then crossed at mile 5.3 and there is a large tree across the creek a little ways downstream that will help you avoid fording at this time.

Now the trail becomes more interesting as it climbs up the lushly vegetated canyon deeply cut in volcanic rock*. Rockhounds have found good samples of agate along Turkey Creek's canyon. At mile 7.5 the trail levels out briefly and crosses Turkey Creek. Climbing up the left side of the canyon, it then passes around some pretty, but marshy meadows and recrosses Turkey Creek. As you proceed up the trail there are some extremely beautiful falls on the creek below you. After climbing steeply the trail reaches a junction where Fourmile Creek Trail (No. 35) is met at mile 9.0. About .5 mile along Fourmile Creek Trail is Turkey Creek Lake (11,135'). Climbing up the mountainside through some switchbacks and downed timber, Turkey Creek Trail soon enters a small basalt-rimmed basin and climbs up to a pass (elevation 11,880') at mile 10.0 where the view is very good. From left to right you see Red Mountain (12,630'), the strangely jutting South River Peak (13,149'), Table Mountain (12,688'), Sawtooth Mountain (12,605'), and Hope Mountain (12,834').

Now above timberline, the trail more or less contours around three basins with big sheer-sided summits above that comprise the headwaters of Rainbow Creek. In the third basin the trail passes under Puerto Blanco (12,620') and at mile 12.5 a spectacular waterfall comes right from the top of this mountain. Ahead is the

---

*People in the area claim to have found some Spanish blazes on trees in Turkey Creek. Legend has it that the Spanish explorers ascended to the Continental Divide via Turkey Creek, branching off from the Spanish Trail which was commonly known to have skirted the foothills by the south of the San Juan Mountains.

white porphyry ridge separating Rainbow and Puerto Blanco Creeks which is the White Door (Puerto Blanco). One of the most interesting aspects of this trail are the colors of white, red, yellow and black rocks and soils that can be seen on the mountains and ridges. Continuing on around the grassy flanks of Red Mountain (12,630'), watch carefully as this is a likely place to see a herd of elk.

The trail climbs and reaches a saddle (mile 13.0) between two of the summits of sprawling Red Mountain and then contours around the steep headwall of Cimarron (Spanish: wild and untamed) Creek's basin. At mile 14.7 another saddle is reached where a number of switchbacks begin the descent to the East Fork of the Piedra River. After the switchbacks the trail enters a section of trees where the going is very slow due to the blow-downs. But finally at mile 17.0 the trail enters the meadows along the river. A spacious park tucked away in rugged mountains is always a delightful change of terrain. This is an ideal place to spend several enjoyable days in a remote section of the Wilderness.

Following some post-markers through the meadows and across the river at mile 17.2, you find a trail junction near the mouth of a small valley. A manway climbs up the little valley to meet the Middle Fork Trail (No. 33) just south of Palomino Mountain (12,230'). Or, you can proceed up along the west side of the East Fork of the Piedra River for 1.4 more miles to reach the Continental Divide Trail (No. 59) and the West Fork Trail (No. 38) at mile 18.6 on Piedra Pass* (11,400').

NO. 38 — WEST FORK TRAIL — — — (Trailhead R)

Trailhead elevation   —   8,080'
Total vertical ascent   —   3,680'
Highest point   —   11,760'
Total vertical descent —   400'
Length — 11.75 miles one way
Maps — 15' Wolf Creek Pass
          15' Spar City
          San Juan National Forest

---

*Formerly Red Mountain Pass but renamed Piedra Pass by the U.S.G.S. on the new 7½' quadrangle of the area.

To reach the West Fork Trailhead drive northeast on Highway 160 from Pagosa Springs toward Wolf Creek Pass for 15.0 miles and turn left on Forest Service Road No. 684 that goes to the Wolf Creek and West Fork Campgrounds. Past the West Fork Campground the road crosses the West Fork of the San Juan River at mile 17.5 and becomes rougher and sometimes muddy as you drive to the West Fork trailhead (R) at mile 20.8.

The West Fork Trail is maintained little if at all and is used primarily by fishermen with some backpack traffic up to the hot springs at mile 4.7. From the hot springs to the Continental Divide the trail is nearly a manway with big trees across it that must be constantly crawled over or circumvented.

From the trailhead you walk on the road for .5 mile to where the trail goes right and passes Borns Lake private resort. At mile 1.5 the trail crosses a bridge over Burro Creek and continues to mile 2.9 where a crossing of the West Fork of the San Juan is made. Before the spring run-off has ended (normally sometime in early July) this crossing may be too difficult. If the river looks big but passable get a strong stick to make a third point of stability during the crossing and be sure you can easily free yourself of your backpack if you go down in the water. Continuing on, the trail soon crosses Beaver Creek, in some ways a more difficult crossing than the San Juan because of rounded mossy rocks. There is a large fallen tree that can be found a little ways downstream and used as a bridge.

The vegetation in the canyon is profuse and especially notable is the size of some of the conifers. At mile 4.25 the trail meets and passes Beaver Creek Trail (No. 39). The hot springs are reached at mile 4.7, a reminder that this area was a volcanic holocaust about 50 million years ago. The canyon widens briefly where Rainbow and Cimarron Creeks join the West Fork of the San Juan and another crossing is made at mile 5.25. At this crossing look up-canyon and notice spectacular waterfalls. The trail now gains elevation with many steep switchbacks. After coming around a ridge point it resumes its ascent of the West Fork. The canyon is now most impressive, one-half mile deep by one and a half miles wide at the top. The dense forest allows only occasional rays of sunlight to filter down and bird calls seem to echo eerily from

the contorted volcanic walls*. The trail is marked by red-painted
strips of metal nailed on trees from time to time. You will rely on
these markers more as you proceed. At mile 8.25 the trail crosses
the San Juan again and the next 1.0 mile goes through meadows
that relieve the domination of the dark canyon somewhat. Several
important tributaries are crossed as you near the headwaters of the
river. At mile 10.75 the trail attains a low point (11,760') on the
ridge between the West Fork of the San Juan and East Fork of the
Piedra and then begins to descend. Watch for post-markers in the
meadows on top and then blazes where you enter the trees. There
is a lot of blown-down timber. The trail comes out of the trees at a
primitive ditch which you follow for .25 mile to meet the Continental Divide Trail (No. 59) and Turkey Creek Trail (No. 37) at
Piedra Pass (11,400'; for note on Piedra Pass, see trail No. 37).
The West Fork Trail combined with Turkey Creek Trail is sometimes called the Rainbow Trail by the Forest Service. The primitive
ditch and other related water works at Piedra Pass take water from
the East Fork of the Piedra across the Continental Divide to empty
into Red Mountain Creek. As a result, an ugly scar is present at
this otherwise beautiful alpine setting.

NO. 39 — BEAVER CREEK TRAIL

Trailhead elevation   —   9,040'
Total vertical ascent —   2,960'
Highest point   —   12,000'
Total vertical descent —   240'
Length   —   9.5 miles one way
Maps — 15' Wolf Creek Pass
         15' Spar City
         San Juan National Forest

Beaver Creek Trail is found at mile 4.25 of the West Fork
Trail (No. 38). This trail is not maintained on a regular basis and is
rapidly deteriorating to a manway. The trail begins with many

---

*Surveyors of the Hayden survey party explored the San Juans in the
mid-1870's. The atlas that resulted from the explorations had given the
present-day West Fork of the San Juan the more descriptive name of Cañon
Creek.

switchbacks which climb over a ridge between the West Fork of the San Juan and Beaver Creek. At mile 2.0, the trail is in Beaver Creek's canyon which is every bit as notable as the magnificent West Fork canyon. Soon it is traversing along the steep mountainside above Beaver Creek which is kept sparsely vegetated by rock and snowslides. A little before mile 5.0 the trail crosses Beaver Creek and soon enters Beaver Meadows (elevation 10,000'). Beaver Meadows is bordered with tall stately spruces and has an air of hushed solitude about it, hidden away in a corner of the Continental Divide. At the upper end of Beaver Meadows the trail turns right to ascend the left side of Elk Creek, climbing steeply at first and then reaching timberline by about mile 8.75. The trail is faint through the tundra with only a few post-markers to guide you until the end at mile 9.5 at a low point on the Continental Divide (12,000'). Here the Continental Divide Trail (No. 59) is met and there is only a small sign that says: Trail 1560, to indicate where Beaver Creek Trail is located. In the summer of 1975, the sign looked as though it wouldn't be standing for long. To the east across a glacial cirque is Sawtooth Mountain (12,605'), named for its south serrated ridge. Hope Mountain (12,834') rises from the Continental Divide 1.5 miles to the southeast.

IV.
South Fork
of the Rio Grande Country

	trailhead	length
No. 40 — Archuleta Lake Trail	(T)	6.5 miles
No. 41 — South Fork of the Rio Grande Trail (Manway)		4.0 miles
No. 42 — Hope Creek Trail	(U)	6.0 miles
No. 43 — Highline Trail	(V)	6.25 miles

22.75 miles

This group of trails is situated just north of Wolf Creek Pass in the South Fork of the Rio Grande drainage. They ascend through beautiful heavy spruce forest and upon reaching the Continental Divide, afford marvelous views. The access is easy and usually few people are encountered in this section.

NO. 40 — ARCHULETA LAKE TRAIL — — — (Trailhead T)

Trailhead elevation — 9,280'
Total vertical ascent — 2,480'
Highest point — 11,760'
Length — 6.5 miles one way
Maps — 15' Spar City
      Rio Grande National Forest
      Rio Grande National Forest Trail No. 839

This trail begins with what was the old South Fork of the Rio Grande Trail. It has been rerouted to follow Archuleta Creek from mile 4.2 with additional changes in the trail below this point. The U.S.G.S. 15' quadrangle does not show Big Meadows Reservoir and depicts only a portion of the trail correctly.

To reach the trailhead (T) of Archuleta Lake Trail drive

Weminuche Wilderness

Hunter Lake

Shaw Lake

BIG MEADOWS RES.

Wolf Cr. Pass

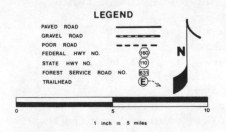

LEGEND

PAVED ROAD	
GRAVEL ROAD	
POOR ROAD	
FEDERAL HWY NO.	(160)
STATE HWY NO.	(110)
FOREST SERVICE ROAD NO.	(631)
TRAILHEAD	(E)

N

0   5   10

1 inch = 5 miles

25.0 miles northeast from Pagosa Springs on Highway 160 to the summit of Wolf Creek Pass. It is then 7.5 miles down the other side to find Forest Service Road No. 410 going left just after Highway 160 crosses the South Fork of the Rio Grande. Forest Service Road No. 410 is also 12.2 miles from South Fork, Colorado, driving southwest on Highway 160. A little over 1.0 mile up road No. 410 the road divides: left to Big Meadows Campground; right to the boat ramps and Elk Creek Road No. 430. Go right and proceed to the boat ramps parking area which is the trailhead (T).

Archuleta Lake Trail begins by skirting the northwest shoreline of Big Meadows Reservoir until reaching the meadows above the lake at mile 1.0. The U.S.G.S. quadrangle shows the trail crossing the South Fork here but this is incorrect. The trail continues along the right of the South Fork of the Rio Grande, enters the forest and climbs as the canyon closes in. Although the South Fork is not the largest stream in the Weminuche Wilderness, it is possibly the most beautiful. The water is constantly descending 3' or 4' falls to swirl and linger in limpid, rock-bound pools. The forest cover is dense and there are few opportunities for a campsite until higher up on Archuleta Creek.

At mile 3.0 after crossing Archuleta Creek, the trail turns right, switchbacks and contours up the steep canyon until mile 4.2. Here Archuleta Creek's canyon has leveled out considerably and the South Fork of the Rio Grande manway (No. 41) goes left across Archuleta Creek. Archuleta Creek Trail now proceeds along the north side of the creek through large meadows that extend up the mountainside on the right to end at Mt. Hope (12,834').

At mile 6.0 the trail crosses Archuleta Creek and enters the timber to climb steeply to Archuleta Lake (11,680') at mile 6.5. The Continental Divide Trail (No. 59) can be seen where it contours around Archuleta Lake's basin to the west. Archuleta Lake has a washed-out (in 1944) dam across the outlet and it is evident that the lake's water level was once somewhat higher. Spotted Lake is .75 mile south along the Continental Divide Trail.

NO. 41 – SOUTH FORK OF THE RIO GRANDE TRAIL
(Manway)

Trailhead elevation   –   10,400'
Total vertical ascent   –   1,200'
Highest point   –   11,280'
Total vertical descent –   340'
Length –   4.0 miles one way
Maps – 15' Spar City
        Rio Grande National Forest
        Rio Grande National Forest Trail No. 750

The South Fork of the Rio Grande Manway, once an important trail to the Continental Divide, is now little used and not maintained. The trail begins at mile 4.2 on Archuleta Lake Trail (No. 40).

After crossing Archuleta Creek the trail ascends a ridge between South Fork and Archuleta Creek canyons. Descending the Rio Grande side through much fallen timber is the most difficult part of the entire manway until at mile 1.0 when the bottom of the canyon is reached. The trail is good at times and at other times faint and easy to lose. Watch for blazed trees for guidance. The canyon runs parallel to the Continental Divide which is situated to the south, and is generally heavily forested with adequate camping. The trail passes through several meadows and it is here that the trail is faintest. The U.S.G.S. 15' quadrangle shows the meadows and trail relationships correctly and will be of some assistance. The last meadow where the South Fork is crossed has a few post-markers and cairns. At mile 4.0 where the trail meets the Continental Divide Trail (No. 59) and ends, there is a dilapidated sign that says: 8 – Twin Bridges. The South Fork Trail used to begin at Highway 160, where Forest Service Road No. 410 now turns off to go to Big Meadows Reservoir. Years ago the highway crossed the South Fork of the Rio Grande on twin bridges at this point.

It is improbable that you would meet anyone on this manway. The terrain is not too difficult to travel and if you possess some map-reading skills and a sharp eye for trail signs you may enjoy this isolated canyon a great deal.

NO. 42 — HOPE CREEK TRAIL — — — (Trailhead U)

Trailhead elevation   —   9,680'
Total vertical ascent —   2,400'
Highest point   —   12,080'
Length —   6.0 miles one way
Maps — 15' Spar City
       Rio Grande National Forest
       Rio Grande National Forest Trail No. 838

To find the trailhead (U) for Hope Creek Trail follow the directions given for Archuleta Lake Trail (No. 40). Instead of stopping at the boat ramps at Big Meadows Reservoir, keep right on Forest Service Road No. 430 (Elk Creek Road) and at about mile 2.5 from Highway 160, find the Hope Creek trailhead (U) where the road crosses Hope Creek and on the right side. Parking your vehicle is a problem here.

The Forest Service map incorrectly shows Hope Creek Trail beginning on the left side of Hope Creek. Climbing only a leisurely 800' in the first 3.0 miles the trail passes through a beautiful canyon with spruce-aspen forest interspersed with meadows. There are views to summits above the canyon, unnamed with the exception of the light-colored Mount Hope (12,834') which is close to the canyon's head. Finally at a little past mile 3.0 the trail turns right to follow a fork of Hope Creek and begins to climb steeply with switchbacks. At mile 4.2 it levels off and crosses the stream in a meadow. Climbing more and a little ways further, the stream is crossed once again and the trail ascends with many switchbacks to a basin above timberline on the east side of Sawtooth Mountain (12,605'). You will find a fine, cold spring upon entering the basin and while getting a drink you may get a look at a Clark's nutcracker on the nearby scrub firs. The Highline Trail (No. 43) contours around the head of this basin and Hope Creek Trail climbs left (south) up a ridge to meet it at mile 6.0 The Highline Trail meets the Continental Divide Trail (No. 59) about .75 mile south of this point.

NO. 43 — HIGHLINE TRAIL — — — (Trailhead V)

Trailhead elevation   —   11,440'
Total vertical ascent   —   1,600'
Highest point   —   12,480'
Total vertical descent —   857'
Length   —   6.25 miles one way
(from Hunter's Lake to Continental Divide)
Maps — 15' Spar City
        Rio Grande National Forest
        Rio Grande National Forest Trail No. 832

The trailhead (V) for the portion of the Highline Trail entering the Wilderness is found by going up Forest Service Road No. 430 (Elk Creek Road) as described in Trail No. 40. Drive by the boat ramps and continue on No. 430 passing Shaw Lake at mile 4.0 and until about mile 10.0 where you will find the Hunter's Lake trailhead (V) and a parking area. Since it is not easy to find water on the Highline Trail until mile 5.5 you may want to bring along a canteen.

At mile .5 the trail goes by Hunter's Lake (11,383') which is man-made and visited by quite a few fishermen with the new road so close by. Past Hunter's Lake in a meadow which shows signs of being an old burned area, the Highline Trail is met by Lake Creek Trail at mile 1.2. Still in meadows the trail climbs a bit, enters a basin and becomes somewhat obscure. A trail going left across the basin leads to an old hunting camp but you must locate a couple of rock cairns and go straight ahead. The trail soon enters a stand of trees as it ascends a steep mountainside and at mile 2.0 reaches the top of the ridge just below the north side of Table Mountain. Here, also, you meet a branch of the Highline Trail that bypassed Hunter's Lake along the ridge above the lake. The trail then climbs up the edge of Table Mountain past the rough and protruding volcanic rock layers known as the "stairsteps".

Table Mountain (12,688') is a vast expanse of tundra and blue sky: an incredible alpine experience with views across the Weminuche Wilderness to the west with South River Peak (13,149') prominent and the Rio Grande Pyramid (12,821') about 30 air miles away. Looking east, you may be able to see the Sangre de Cristo Mountain Range across the San Luis Valley some 70 air miles distant.   Across Table Mountain the trail consists of rock cairns spaced out over the tundra and at mile 3.25 the Table Mountain Trail is met. This trail goes over the eastern side of Table Mountain to end at Shaw Lake in 8.0 miles after traveling through a timber sale.

There always seem to be a few flocks of ptarmigan on Table Mountain which are particularly easy to observe if the weather is inclement. As the trail goes south, Table Mountain narrows (mile 4.0) and there are good views of a side canyon of Hope Creek on the left and into upper Goose Creek on the right. After going right of a 12,688' gently sloping summit, the trail begins descending into a basin to pass around the craggy Sawtooth Mountain (12,605'). Here it meets Hope Creek Trail (No. 42) at mile 5.5. A little ways into the basin down Hope Creek Trail, water can be found. Continuing on around the east side of Sawtooth Mountain the trail climbs and meets the Continental Divide Trail (No. 59) at mile 6.25.

V.

In the Bend

	trailhead	length
No. 44 — Goose Creek Trail (upper)		.5.5 miles
No. 45 — Sawtooth Trail.		.3.5 miles
No. 46 — Fisher Creek Trail.	(W & X)	.2.7 miles
No. 47 — Trout Creek Trail	(Y)	.9.0 miles
No. 48 — East Trout Creek Trail (manway)		.7.0 miles
No. 49 — Fern Creek Stock Driveway . . .	(Z)	.7.75 miles
No. 50 — Texas Creek Trail	(AA)	.11.0 miles
No. 51 — Squaw Creek Trail	(BB)	.9.25 miles
No. 52 — Squaw Lake Trail		.3.75 miles

59.45 miles

"In the Bend" refers to the section of the Wilderness north of the Continental Divide where it runs from west to east before resuming its southerly trend which is found through most of Colorado. These mountains are essentially volcanic but not as obvious as section III. The finer layered volcanic deposits are on top of the high smooth ridges characteristic of these mountains.

There is a problem or two with access at certain points. The need for water in the San Luis Valley downstream on the Rio Grande has resulted in some small water projects (mostly of 1930 vintage) that mark the Wilderness here and there. There is quite a bit of commercial grazing around trails No. 49 and No. 50. Up near the Continental Divide the mountains are rough and spectacular and few if any people are encountered.

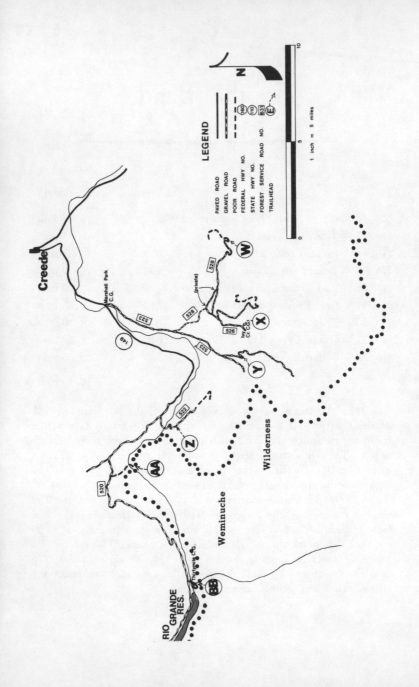

LEGEND

PAVED ROAD

GRAVEL ROAD

POOR ROAD

FEDERAL HWY NO. (160)

STATE HWY NO. (110)

FOREST SERVICE ROAD NO. 631

TRAILHEAD (E)

1 inch = 5 miles

0   5   10

N

Creede

Marshall Park C.G.

149

523

528

528   (private)

526   hwy Ck. C.G.

X

W

Y

522

Z

AA

520

Thirtymile C.G.

BB

RIO GRANDE RES.

Weminuche   Wilderness

NO. 44 – GOOSE CREEK TRAIL (upper)

Trailhead elevation   —   12,400'
Total vertical descent —   2,200'
Highest point   —   12,400'
Length —   5.5 miles one way
Maps — 15' Spar City
        Rio Grande National Forest
        Rio Grande National Forest Trail No. 827

Goose Creek is one of the largest drainages on the Rio Grande side of the Continental Divide. It begins at South River Peak and empties into the Rio Grande at Wagon Wheel Gap. Because of private holdings from Wagon Wheel Gap to about eight miles up the valley, the normal trailhead is not available to the public. Therefore the guidebook will deal only with the last 5.5 miles of Goose Creek's Trail. The trail will be described from the top where it meets Fisher Creek Trail (No. 46) by Little Goose Lake, down to the junction with Sawtooth Trail (No. 45), close to the Wilderness boundary.

Where Fisher Creek Trail has passed Little Goose Lake and climbed to about 100 yards east, the beginning of Goose Creek Trail can be found. After walking northeast along a fairly level bench for about .4 mile past a few cairns, the trail suddenly begins the steep descent into Goose Creek's basin. As it descends, the trail swings back right (south) toward the head of the basin and passes many strong elk trails which can easily get you confused. Soon the trail reaches a small stream, continues down along its left and begins leveling off at mile 1.2 after about 1,000' of vertical descent.

The walls of the basin rise spectacularly in dark cliffs up to South River Peak (13,149') with several droning waterfalls. It is obvious that the basin is large, but if you see backpackers or horses which appear very tiny when crossing the trail 1,500' above you and just below South River Peak, you will begin to realize the scale on which nature exists in the Wilderness.

At mile 1.5 Goose Creek is crossed for the first time and the trail enters the forest. Goose Creek Trail is generally distinct but little used. Between this point and Sawtooth Trail at mile 5.5 the valley parallels the Continental Divide and is a constant alternation of forest and meadow. Large herds of elk graze in Goose Creek throughout the summer and you may be able to see them if you approach the meadows cautiously. At mile 3.4 Goose Creek is crossed and then two more crossings follow within the next .5 mile. At mile 5.5 there is a good Forest Service sign that directs you to Sawtooth Trail (No. 45) which ascends in 3.5 miles to the Continental Divide after a crossing of Goose Creek.

Upper Goose Creek because of the difficult access is a very isolated but splendid valley in which one could enjoy several days of studying nature and exploring.

NO. 45 — SAWTOOTH TRAIL

Trailhead elevation   —   10,200'
Total vertical ascent —   1,880'
Highest point   —   12,080'
Length —   3.5 miles one way
Maps — 15' Spar City
              Rio Grande National Forest
              Rio Grande National Forest Trail No. 828

The Sawtooth Trail exists primarily as a connecting trail between Goose Creek Trail (No. 44) and the Continental Divide Trail (No. 59). It ascends a steep, unnamed tributary of Goose Creek with little possibility of camping along the way. The trail is not maintained but every three or four years. If the weather is rainy, Sawtooth Trail becomes a quagmire of black, sticky mud.

At mile 1.5 where the trail levels off a bit and enters a small meadow, the U.S.G.S. 15' quadrangle shows the trail incorrectly continuing along the creek. As shown in the guidebook's map, the trail switches back once to climb along the mountain side before reaching the basin below the Divide. Here again the 15' quadrangle depicts the trail incorrectly and after about seven switchbacks the Continental Divide Trail (No. 59) is reached at mile 3.5.

The Sawtooth Trail along with Goose Creek Trail and the necessary part of Fisher Creek Trail make an interesting 10.5 mile digression from the Continental Divide Trail.

NO. 46 — FISHER CREEK TRAIL — — — (Trailheads W and X,
        see explanation)

Trailhead elevation   —   11,760' (at Goose Lake)
Total vertical ascent —   1,120'
Highest point   —   12,880'
Total vertical descent —   240'
Length —   2.7 miles one way
(from Goose Lake to Continental Divide)
Maps — 15' Spar City
        Rio Grande National Forest
        Rio Grande National Forest Trail No. 826

    Only at the very end of Fisher Creek Trail is the Weminuche
Wilderness reached. Fisher Creek Trail in entirety is not a practical
approach to the Weminuche except for the last 2.7 miles where it
passes Goose Lake and then Little Goose Lake on the way to the
Continental Divide.
    There are two trailheads which provide access to Goose Lake
and the final 2.7 miles of Fisher Creek Trail: Trailhead X for Ivy
Creek Trail, or Trailhead W at the North Lime Trailhead for Deep
Creek Trail. To reach these trailheads drive 7.0 miles southwest
from Creede on State Highway 149 to the second bridge over the
Rio Grande and just before crossing, find Forest Service Middle
Creek Road (No. 523) and turn left. At mile 11.0 from Creede
turn onto Forest Service Lime Creek Road (No. 528). Finally at
14.5 (from Creede) Lime Creek Road meets Red Mountain Creek
Road. Here you can drive left for 5.5 miles to the North Lime
trailhead (W) or onto Red Mountain Creek Road (No. 526) for 2.0
miles to reach Ivy Creek Campground and Ivy Creek trailhead (X).
Red Mountain Creek Road soon becomes rough but remains
passable for passenger cars. There is an Ivy Creek Road which
turns left from Red Mountain Creek Road; do not take it!

DEEP CREEK TRAIL—(Trailhead W)   IVY CREEK TRAIL—(Trailhead X)

Trailhead elevation	—	10,720'	Trailhead elevation	—	9,200'
Total vertical ascent	—	1,880'	Total vertical ascent	—	2,400'
Highest point	—	12,600'	Highest point	—	11,600'
Total descent	—	1,000'	Length	—	9.0 miles one way

Length — 7.75 miles one way
(then 2.25 miles on Ivy Creek Trail
to meet Fisher Creek Trail)
Rio Grande National Forest Trail
No. 806

Length — 9.0 miles one way
(Deep Creek Trail meets Ivy Creek
Trail at mile 6.5)
Rio Grande National Forest Trail
No. 805

Deep Creek Trail has 520' less vertical ascent than Ivy Creek Trail but has 1,000' of vertical descent enroute. Deep Creek Trail crosses the gently rolling Fisher Mountain (12,857') and commands superb views of the area. Personally I choose this trail to reach Goose Lake, Fisher Creek Trail and the Weminuche Wilderness if the weather looks fair for traveling over the high exposed section on Fisher Mountain.

Ivy Creek Trail climbs a steep 2,400' in the the first 6.5 miles with little inspiring scenery. At mile 6.5 Deep Creek Trail from trailhead W ends and Ivy Creek Trail continues for 2.5 miles more to Goose Lake and Fisher Creek Trail at the south end of the lake. Goose Lake (11,760') is a man-raised lake and has plenty of camping space but looks somewhat used.

Ivy Creek Trail would be a good alternative to Deep Creek Trail if it is a time of thunderstorms.

The final 2.7 miles of Fisher Creek Trail from its junction with Ivy Creek Trail at the south end of Goose Lake passes Little Goose Lake at mile 1.0. Between Goose and Little Goose Lakes, the trail is shown incorrectly on the U.S.G.S. 15' quadrangle. It angles right to climb and contour above cliffs to reach Little Goose Lake. The route shown on the U.S.G.S. map that stays close to the creek goes through bogs and wet meadows. Little Goose Lake (12,160') is above timberline and lies in a basin beneath South River Peak. Beautiful Mountain (12,753') lies northeast. The camping around Little Goose Lake is limited because the basin slopes upward with sliderock and ends in the sheer cliffs of South River Peak. There are a few small spots, however, that would be adequate for someone whose equipment can withstand the weather extremes above timberline.

After crossing the creek from Little Goose Lake and going a little uphill, Goose Creek Trail (No. 44) is found at mile 1.2. At the risk of creating more confusion let me point out that Goose

Lake and Little Goose Lake are not on the Goose Creek drainage; rather, they drain into Fisher Creek. Your trail continues southwest ascending a steep ridge to pass just below South River Peak (13,149'). The view is tremendous. Looking west, a large part of the Weminuche Wilderness is laid out before you and perhaps you can even see as far as the La Plata Mountain Range on the other side of Durango, 60 air miles away. To the east, over 80 air miles away and across the San Luis Valley, you may be able to see the Sangre de Cristo Mountain Range. The Continental Divide Trail (No. 59) is met at mile 2.7.

NO. 47 — TROUT CREEK TRAIL — — — (Trailhead Y)

Trailhead elevation   —   9,400'
Total vertical ascent   —   2,920'
Highest point   —   11,960'
Total vertical descent — 320'
Length — 9.0 miles one way
Maps — 7½' Workman Creek
            7½' Little Squaw Creek
            Rio Grande National Forest
            Rio Grande National Forest Trail No. 811

To reach the trailhead (Y) for Trout Creek Trail drive 7.0 miles southwest from Creede on State Highway 149 to the second bridge over the Rio Grande. Forest Service Middle Creek Road (No. 523) turns left just before the bridge. Continue on Middle Creek Road past Lime Creek Road at mile 11.0 to mile 15.5 (from Creede). Here the road has just begun to climb up the mountain to Love Lake and the trailhead (Y) is located right at the corner of the first switchback.

This trailhead was constructed to create an access on National Forest land around the private holdings which are situated at the mouth of Trout Creek. After 2.0 miles the trail crosses Trout Creek and proceeds upstream on the old jeep road that serves as a trail from this point. The trail crosses Trout Creek many times, and the snowmelt during the early summer may make Trout Creek swollen and difficult to ford. The canyon narrows quickly after mile 2.0 until about mile 3.75 where a jeep road (now closed) descends to the Wilderness from Copper Creek and Middle Creek Road. The trail follows the jeep road until mile 5.0 where, in the meadows about 250 yards above the junction of Trout and East Trout Creeks, the trail turns 90 degrees to the right. The jeep road continues on up East Trout Creek to become the East Trout Creek Manway (No. 48).

Trout Creek is crossed again leaving the jeep roads behind and begins climbing steeply at about mile 6.0. The trail is in forest but you soon will be able to see Middle Trout Creek's canyon on the left. Continuing very steep until mile 7.25, the trail levels off in a meadow below the Knife Edge, a jagged, narrow ridge of volcanic rock 1,000' above you, that juts out from the Continental Divide. Leaving the meadow the trail rises steeply to ascend volcanic layers of the same composition as the Knife Edge and at mile 8.0 a trail goes left to climb around and up the Knife Edge meeting the Continental Divide Trail (No. 59) in .75 mile. At mile 8.25, by man-raised Trout Lake (11,685') Texas Creek Trail (No. 50) is met. Continuing on past Trout Lake to the open, rolling divide between Trout and Williams Creek Lakes, the Continental Divide Trail is reached at mile 9.0. Williams Lake Trail (No. 29) descends to Williams Lake and on to Williams Creek.

Camping around Trout and Williams Lakes is above timberline and requires high altitude tents and backpacking stoves. After the junction at mile 5.0 Trout Creek Trail is very scenic and interesting. Traveling on the old jeep roads and past other marks of man to get to that point may be aesthetically unacceptable to some.

NO. 48 — EAST TROUT CREEK TRAIL — (Manway)

Trailhead elevation   —   9,400'
Total vertical ascent —   3,080'
Highest point   —   12,040'
Total vertical descent —   280'
Length   —   7.0 miles one way
Maps — 7½' Workman Creek
             7½' Palomino Mountain
             Rio Grande National Forest
             Rio Grande National Forest Trail No. 810

The East Trout Creek Manway is found at mile 5.0 on Trout Creek Trail (No. 47). Trout Creek Trail turns right at this point and the East Trout Creek Manway (in the form of an old jeep road) continues ahead crossing East Trout Creek at mile .5 and climbing to the sulphur mine at mile 1.0. The old mine is shown on a 1905 map of the region and has had no recent development.

The trail continues on to the Continental Divide Trail at mile 7.0. The Forest Service has made plans to improve East Trout Creek Trail but presently it is in very bad shape. Continual downed timber across the trail, one stream crossing after another through heavy forest and almost no suitable campsites tells the story for this trail. It is not recommended for travel until after the reconstruction planned by the Forest Service.

NO. 49 — FERN CREEK STOCK DRIVEWAY — — — (Trailhead Z)

Trailhead elevation   —   9,236'
Total vertical ascent   —   2,682'
Highest point   —   11,558'
Total vertical descent —   1,671'
Length   —   7.75 miles one way
(to Little Squaw Creek)
Maps —   7½' Workman Creek
             7½' Little Squaw Creek
             Rio Grande National Forest
             Rio Grande National Forest Trail No. 815

With some exceptions, active stock driveways such as the Fern Creek Driveway are usually not satisfactory backpacking trails. The primary reason for their existence is movement of sheep or cattle through the mountains. Steepness of ascent or descent along driveway routes is not considered or reduced by switchbacks since the animals are usually driven the shortest distance betweeen two points barring natural obstacles. The Fern Creek Driveway is very steep and, after mile 7.75 (Little Squaw Creek), it is badly deteriorated and shown (but not described) on the guidebook's map as a manway to Squaw Creek (mile 13.0). The Forest Service map shows the Fern Creek Driveway continuing from Squaw Creek to Weminuche Creek. The only thing that resembles a trail in this section are occasional yellow markers nailed to trees across extremely difficult terrain on an improbable route.

Drive southwest from Creede on State Highway 149 (paving ends about mile 13.5) for 17.3 miles to reach Forest Service Fern Creek Road (No. 522). This road turns left from the highway, crosses the Rio Grande and climbs to the trailhead (Z) in 1.8 miles.

After a few switchbacks the trail soon enters Fern Creek's canyon and climbs steeply along Fern Creek until mile 3.2 at Little Ruby Lake (11,200'). Here, also, Texas Creek Trail (No. 50) joins the Fern Creek Driveway for a short time. Over a low ridge Fuchs Reservoir (11,260') is reached at mile 3.75. The Texas Creek Trail goes left to reach Ruby Lake (11,290') in .4 mile. Fuchs Reservoir and Ruby Lakes are visited frequently by fishermen and have a somewhat messy appearance. The Fern Creek Driveway descends to the meadows of Texas Creek and crosses at mile 4.5. There are considerable numbers of stock grazing in the vicinity and it would probably be wise to consider their position when finding drinking water along this trail. Now the trail climbs to a wide pass (11,558') between the Texas Creek and Little Squaw Creek drainages and at about mile 6.5 begins a headlong descent (18% grade) into Little Squaw Creek. Little Squaw Creek is trailless but there are almost continuous meadows along the creek to the upper end at the Continental Divide. Some not too difficult cross-country walking could take you to the very beautiful and wild country approximately 3.0 to 4.0 miles upstream.

NO. 50 — TEXAS CREEK TRAIL — — — (Trailhead AA)

Trailhead elevation   —   9,015'
Total vertical ascent —   4,240'
Highest point   —   12,280'
Total vertical descent —   1,000'
Length   —   11.0 miles one way
Maps — 15' Bristol Head
        7½' Little Squaw Creek
        7½' Workman Creek
        Rio Grande National Forest
        Rio Grande National Forest Trail No. 816

Drive southwest from Creede on State Highway 149 for 21.4 miles (the last 8.0 miles on gravel) to a junction where you then turn left on Forest Service Road No. 520 toward Rio Grande Reservoir. Right goes to Spring Creek and Slumgullion Passes. At mile 22.5 you will notice a road on the left with a gate and.a "no trespassing" sign. It is then 1.5 miles up this rough dirt road to the summer home group where the Texas Creek trailhead is located. The road is on private property but the Forest Service maintains public access to the trailhead. After crossing the Rio Grande turn right for about 200 yards to reach the trailhead (AA).

After climbing 800' and out of the Rio Grande's canyon, Texas Creek Trail descends briefly to cross Texas Creek at mile 1.75, then resumes the ascent, becoming very steep until about 3.0. The trail then crosses a broad ridge to meet the Fern Creek Stock Driveway (No. 49) at mile 4.5. The Fern Creek Stock Driveway has climbed from the more accessible trailhead Z in 3.2 miles to reach this point and is a better alternative if Ruby Lakes and country south is your objective. There is considerable commercial grazing in the Texas Creek and Ruby Lakes vicinity.

The trail continues around the east end of Little Ruby Lake (11,200') to climb a low ridge and then descends to Fuchs Reservoir (11,260') at mile 5.3. Here the Fern Creek Driveway turns right toward Texas Creek. Meanwhile, Texas Creek Trail passes close to the western end of Fuchs Reservoir to reach Ruby Lake (11,290') at mile 5.5 by some herder's cabins. Here, a branch of Texas Creek Trail goes right to descend to Texas Creek. Proceed on around Ruby Lake to the east to climb a meadowed valley leading up to Baldy Mountain (12,488'). Although meadows extend to the summit on the west and south, the north face has been harshly sculpted by glacial ice. Soon timberline and the alpine tundra above is reached. The trail turns southwest to travel along the northwest side of a ridge at an elevation of over 12,000'. Chief Mountain (13,014') can be seen straight ahead as well as several unnamed summits along the Continental Divide to the left. The branch of Texas Creek Trail that descended to Texas Creek at Ruby Lake is soon met and at mile 8.5 the trail passes by Red Lakes, a collection of 12 shallow ponds which make up the head of Texas Creek. Rounding the ridge of a 12,603' summit the trail soon begins to descend steeply into Trout Lake's basin with a good view of the volcanic Knife Edge about 1.5 miles away. Trout Creek Trail (No. 47) is met at mile 11.0, east of 11,685' Trout Lake. The Continental Divide Trail (No. 59) is found .75 mile south at the end of Trout Creek Trail.

NO. 51 — SQUAW CREEK TRAIL — — — (Trailhead BB)

Trailhead elevation   —   9,360'
Total vertical ascent —   1,840'
Highest point   —   11,200'
Length — 9.25 miles one way
Maps — 7½' Weminuche Pass
              7½' Little Squaw Creek
              7½' Cimarrona Peak
              Rio Grande National Forest
              Rio Grande National Forest Trail No. 814

To reach the Squaw Creek Trailhead (BB; also the Weminuche Creek trailhead) drive southwest from Creede on State Highway 149 for 21.4 miles (last 8.0 miles are gravel). Turn left on Forest Service Road No. 520 to the Rio Grande Reservoir. After several lakes the road reaches River Hill (mile 29.25) and begins descending to the Rio Grande canyon. The entrance to the Forest Service Thirtymile Campground is reached at mile 31.75. Across the bridge take the first right turn available and continue on around to a loading chute and parking area. The trailhead (BB) is about 100 yards south at the edge of the forest.

About 50 yards after beginning, Weminuche Creek Trail (No. 53) goes right. Squaw Creek Trail proceeds left into the Squaw Creek canyon which is narrow and heavily forested initially. At .5 mile a bridge crosses Squaw Creek and the trail continues on the east side. The canyon progressively widens into a broad valley with continuous meadow along the creek for its entire length and walls of dark timber rising steeply from both sides. Glacial ice did a thorough job straightening and cutting down to create Squaw Creek's valley.

At mile 2.0 the Fern Creek Stock Driveway (No. 49) goes left (read description before using) to reach Little Squaw Creek, a drainage of almost identical topography to Squaw Creek. Continuing up the valley, the ascent is very gentle and makes for easy, idyllic walking through the extended meadows. Squaw Creek Trail receives quite a bit of use from fishermen and day-hikers over about the first half of the trail.

Close to mile 4.0 you begin seeing Chief Mountain (13,014')
above the valley to the left. The valley walls ascend directly to the
summit in a breath-taking rise of 2,500'. Such steepness naturally
makes prime snowslide slopes and thins the spruces and firs un-
mercifully. The west side of the canyon is indented with numerous glacial cirques. At mile 5.5 the Squaw Creek Trail divides
briefly. The main trail climbs a little to the left on benches above
the creek. Going right along the branch takes you through a boggy
area close to the creek. A crossing follows, making it easy to find
Squaw Lake Trail (No. 52).

Squaw Creek Trail continues and at times becomes indistinct
as it crosses Squaw Creek and follows occasional post-markers. It
climbs to reach Squaw Pass (11,200') at mile 9.25. Here the
Continental Divide Trail (No. 59) and Hossick Creek Trail (No. 25)
are found. Squaw Pass is a good place for camping and sees few
visitors as a general rule.

NO. 52 — SQUAW LAKE TRAIL

Trailhead elevation   —   10,320'
Total vertical ascent —   2,080'
Highest point   —   12,400'
Length —   3.75 miles one way
Maps — 7½' Little Squaw Creek
        7½' Weminuche Pass
        Rio Grande National Forest
        Rio Grande National Forest Trail No. 890

Squaw Lake Trail is scheduled for reconstruction by the
Forest Service. The first 2.5 miles of trail are badly eroded and
covered by large sections of blown-down timber which are almost
impossible to cross. Squaw Lake Trail, complete on the guidebook
map, is not on the U.S.G.S. 7½' quadrangle and is depicted only on
the Forest Service map from Squaw Lake to the Continental Divide.

Squaw Lake Trail begins at about mile 5.5 of Squaw Creek
Trail (No. 51). After crossing to the west side of Squaw Creek the
trail climbs a low bench close to the unnamed creek of a side
canyon. It then begins ascending the unnamed creek's canyon
which is just south of the Squaw Lake drainage. The narrow
canyon will wring the sweat out of you but is impressive with the

south side consisting of dark volcanic cliffs and evidencing a great deal of snowslide activity. When the way has just begun to level off a bit at mile 2.0, the trail switchbacks to cross over into Squaw Lake's cirque and reaches Squaw Lake (11,632') at mile 2.5. Squaw Lake is a man-raised lake and some of the horse-drawn equipment that was used to build the earthen dam in 1938 can be seen lying about. Squaw Lake has satisfactory fishing and camping but looks somewhat used. After the trail reconstruction is complete this will probably be visited frequently by horse parties on day rides from Thirtymile Campground.

The trail crosses the dam and angles northeast climbing steeply to reach the ridge above the cirque in which the lake is located. The Continental Divide Trail (No. 59) is reached at mile 3.75. Fine views are all around for those who take time to walk to the vicinity of the Divide.

VI.

Ute Creeks Country

	trailhead	length
No. 53 — Weminuche Creek Trail	(BB)	5.0 miles
No. 54 — Ute Creek Trail	(CC)	12.0 miles
No. 55 — East Ute Creek Trail		3.5 miles
No. 56 — Ute Lake Trail		2.5 miles
No. 57 — West Ute Lake Trail		1.75 miles
No. 58 — La Garita Stock Driveway (West Ute Creek)		7.1 miles
		31.8 miles

Ute Creeks and Weminuche Creek tucked away in the southwest corner of the Bend are under the shadow of the Rio Grande Pyramid and La Ventana (the Window). There are many miles of wide open meadows along gently ascending valleys and quite a number of lakes near the Continental Divide. With the exception of No. 53, the upper Ute Creeks and adjacent lakes are probably visited as much by people crossing the Divide from section II as from trailheads BB and CC.

NO. 53 — WEMINUCHE CREEK TRAIL — — — (Trailhead BB)
(Rio Grande side)

Trailhead elevation   —   9,360'
Total vertical ascent   —   1,262'
Highest point   —   10,622'
Total vertical descent —   75'
Length —   5.0 miles one way
Maps — 7½' Weminuche Pass
       Rio Grande National Forest
       Rio Grande National Forest Trail No. 818

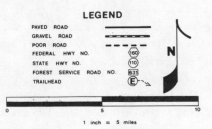

LEGEND

PAVED ROAD	————————
GRAVEL ROAD	– – – – – –
POOR ROAD	- - - - - -
FEDERAL HWY NO.	(160)
STATE HWY NO.	(110)
FOREST SERVICE ROAD NO.	631
TRAILHEAD	(E)

N

1 inch = 5 miles

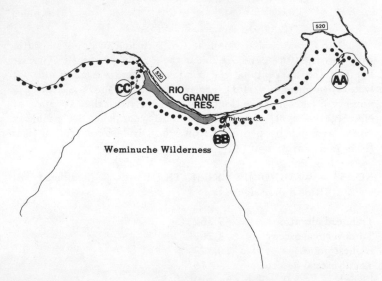

Drive 31.75 miles from Creede to Thirtymile Campground as described in Squaw Creek Trail (No. 51). The trailhead (BB) for Squaw Creek Trail is also the trailhead for Weminuche Creek Trail.

About 50 yards after the trailhead, Squaw Creek and Weminuche Creek Trails separate and Weminuche Creek Trail climbs away to the west to pass by the Rio Grande Reservoir dam and spillway at mile .5. The trail contours around the lake through aspen and begins to climb about mile 1.0. At times, there can be quite a bit of horse traffic along this trail, mostly rental day rides (with inexperienced riders) from the riding stables at the spillway. Also, the trail through this section is narrow at times, so be ready to make any horse-backpacker encounters smooth (see Manners on the Trail). At mile 1.7 the trail turns left into Weminuche Creek's canyon and soon a good view of Rio Grande Reservoir with Pole Creek Mountain (13,716') in the distance is seen. At mile 2.0, after passing through a rockslide area the canyon becomes a gorge and Weminuche Creek is crossed on a bridge. Just before crossing the bridge, you will find a small side creek on the left which makes an excellent cold drink. For a short distance after the bridge the climbing is very hard until the trail leaves the gorge.

The scenery along Weminuche Creek Trail changes suddenly to wide meadows bordered with aspen and a few spruce. The trail stays 250 yards west of Weminuche Creek and about 120 yards above it, making camping not readily available. At mile 4.0 a good-sized side creek which descends from Simpson Mountain is crossed and at mile 4.75 you reach Weminuche Creek. The stream may require fording with shoes and socks off if the snowmelt is still a factor (usually through June). There has been a crude bridge built by hikers but don't count on this being there from year to year. At mile 5.0, Weminuche Pass (10,622') and the headwaters of the Pine River are reached (see Pine River Trail, No. 14, for historical notes about Weminuche Pass). Continuing across the expansive meadows on Weminuche Pass the trail meets the Continental Divide Trail (No. 59) going west up Rincon La Vaca Creek just before crossing Raber Lohr Ditch (about 1.0 mile south of Weminuche Pass). After another .3 mile of walking beyond the ditch, you will find the Continental Divide Trail going left across the meadows to ascend the North Fork of the Pine. Currently there are no signs marking the location of the Divide Trail.

NO. 54 — UTE CREEK TRAIL — — — (Trailhead CC)

Trailhead elevation   —   9,450'
Total vertical ascent   —   2,350'
Highest point   —   11,800'
Total vertical descent —   280'
Length —   12.0 miles one way
Maps — 7½' Finger Mesa
             7½' Rio Grande Pyramid
             Rio Grande National Forest
             Rio Grande National Forest Trail No. 819

Ute Creek Trail is relatively well-known but seldom seems crowded. About 7.5 miles up Ute Creek Trail, the three tributaries of Ute Creek, East Ute, Middle Ute and West Ute Creeks, join to form the main stream. The area of the upper Ute Creeks is a large basin of about 25 square miles bounded by Ute Ridge on the northwest and continuing with the Continental Divide around south and east to Rio Grande Pyramid. Scattered around the edge of the basin along the Continental Divide, Clark Lake, Middle and West Ute Lakes, Twin Lakes, and Ute Lake combined make a total of 84 acres of water. The Continental Divide Trail (No. 59) passes all the lakes and connects all the trails that ascend the three tributaries.

To reach the Ute Creek trailhead (CC) drive 31.75 miles from Creede to the Thirtymile Campground as described in Squaw Creek Trail (No. 51). Continue on the road (Forest Service No. 520) past the campground and along the north side of the Rio Grande Reservoir to mile 37.75 where a short road turns left to the Ute Creek trailhead (CC).

From the parking area it is only about 50 yards to where the Rio Grande must be forded. This could be nearly impossible until mid-summer in years of heavy run-off. The crossing is usually not difficult for backpackers in normal years, however. Once across the Rio Grande, climb to the grassy benches above the river and continue uphill toward the trees. The old Ute Creek Trail will probably be seen where it stays on the benches close to the river and it is not to be taken. Ute Creek Trail enters the trees and contours around to the mouth of Ute Creek's canyon in about 1.0 mile and ascends through aspen and mixed conifer. You may be able to get a glimpse of Simpson Mountain (12,904') above and to the left. The canyon is very rough with heavy forest cover and Ute Creek roaring down through a gorge along the bottom. At mile 3.0 the trail comes to some peculiarly eroded cliffs which protrude out above Ute Creek running about 120' below. Past the cliffs, the trail descends to meadows which have a few good places for campsites although there are also large sections of willows and marsh as well. At mile 4.0 the meadows are left behind and the canyon closes in again until mile 6.5 where Black Lake is reached. Black Lake (10,875') is not very attractive in reality but pictures of it seem to turn out handsomely.

At mile 6.8 the trail leaves the forest and the great meadow at the confluence of Ute Creeks is laid out before you. Take some time to let the scale of this huge park penetrate your senses. At this point the La Garita Stock Driveway (No. 58) begins angling right, toward West Ute Creek. Your trail descends to cross West Ute Creek at mile 7.4 and East Ute Creek Trail (No. 55) turns left at about mile 7.5. Ute Creek Trail continues up Middle Ute Creek with a little climbing and then gradually eases into a spacious meadow of its own. At mile 9.9 Ute Lake Trail (No. 56) goes left and crosses the creek to reach Ute Lake in 2.0 miles. The trail continues, now climbing again, and crosses a good-sized side creek. Soon it is close to Middle Ute Creek while ascending Middle Ute Creek's valley which has narrowed to a ravine. The valley opens again and at mile 11.0 a branch of the trail continues along to the right and climbs in 1.5 miles to the Continental Divide at a point between Middle and West Ute Lakes. The main trail crosses the two streams now making up Ute Creek and after more climbing reaches Twin Lakes (11,792') and the Continental Divide Trail (No. 59) at mile 12.0.

Camping at Twin Lakes is an above timberline affair with little wood for fires and cooking and exposed to any storms that may come along. Use a backpacking stove and high altitude tent.

NO. 55 — EAST UTE CREEK TRAIL

Trailhead elevation   —   10,680'
Total vertical ascent —   1,363'
Highest point   —   12,043'
Length —   3.5 miles one way
Maps — 7½' Rio Grande Pyramid
          Rio Grande National Forest
          Rio Grande National Forest Trail No. 824

East Ute Creek Trail is found at mile 7.5 of Ute Creek Trail (No. 54). Ute Creek Trail has just crossed West Ute Creek and the maps show East Ute Creek Trail beginning by going left and crossing Middle Ute Creek. Actually, you can cross anywhere in this vicinity that looks good, and perhaps even before West Ute Creek, since you may have to take off shoes and socks for the West Ute crossing anyway.

East Ute Creek Trail is faint in the meadows on the other side of the creek and you should watch for a post-marker and blazed trees at mile .5 where the trail enters the timber. After some moderately steep climbing at mile 1.0 the trail enters the meadows that extend two miles up this beautiful gem of a valley. Since there are no lakes on East Ute Creek it is much less visited than the other Ute Creeks and as you continue along you will notice the trail is only a faint path most of the time. From about mile 1.25, walk over towards the creek and enjoy superb views of the Rio Grande Pyramid (13,821') and the Window (La Ventana). In rainy weather East Ute Creek seems to get more than its share, no doubt because of its proximity to that old weather-maker, the Pyramid.

As the trail climbs through the gently sloping valley you will probably see a good many wildflowers. Along the stream, flowers in mid-summer bloom in many-colored profusion. Some that you may see are deep red roseroot, Parry's primrose, and delicate pink paintbrush. Finally at mile 3.0 the meadows end and the trail climbs steeply to reach the Continental Divide Trail (No. 59) at mile 3.5.

The Rio Grande Pyramid

NO. 56 — UTE LAKE TRAIL

Trailhead elevation   —   11,080'
Total vertical ascent —   840'
Highest point   —   11,920'
Length —   2.5 miles one way
Maps — 7½' Rio Grande Pyramid
        Rio Grande National Forest
        Rio Grande National Forest Trail No. 905

    Ute Lake Trail leaves Ute Creek Trail (No. 54) at mile 9.9.
After crossing Middle Ute Creek, Ute Lake Trail ascends a branch
of Middle Ute Creek that comes down from the southeast and Ute
Lake. The trail begins climbing and crosses the small stream, then
soon levels off. At the edge of the meadow (mile 1.4) the trail
climbs again, this time more steeply until at mile 1.75 where
timberline is reached. It then swings right ascending along the
stream coming from Ute Lake. At mile 2.0, Ute Lake is reached.
Continuing around to the east and climbing to the low ridge on the
south, the Continental Divide Trail (No. 59) is met at mile 2.5.
    Ute Lake (11,847') is the largest of the lakes in the area (35
acres) and is set in a rocky, irregular-shaped bowl. There is a little
space to camp on the southwest side but keep in mind that this is
above timberline, requiring certain types of clothing and equipment.
    The U.S.G.S. 7½' quadrangle shows Ute Lake Trail passing
the lake about .25 mile to the east to reach the Continental Divide
Trail. There is an old trail along this route but you can also travel
directly to the outlet of Ute Lake as shown on the guidebook map.

NO. 57 — WEST UTE LAKE TRAIL

Trailhead elevation   —   11,200'
Total vertical ascent —   600'
Highest point   —   11,800'
Length —   1.75 miles one way
Maps — 7½' Rio Grande Pyramid
        Rio Grande National Forest
        Rio Grande National Forest Trail No. 825

West Ute Lake Trail is found on the La Garita Stock Driveway (No. 58) which ascends West Ute Creek. At mile 3.1 of the La Garita Driveway, West Ute Lake Trail turns left and after 150 yards or so crosses a side stream. This side stream empties into West Ute Creek about 100 yards below that point. The trail can probably be seen climbing the bank and low ridge on the opposite side of the side creek.

The trail continues through the meadows of West Ute Creek and is not particularly easy to see although the heavier traffic in recent years has made the trail more visible. At mile 1.1 it crosses West Ute Creek and reaches the timber at mile 1.4. Locate the blazed trees if you are unsure where to enter. After a short but steep climb the Continental Divide Trail (No. 59) is met at mile 1.75, close to the creek and about 100 yards below West Ute Lake (11,801'). This lake may be the prettiest of the Ute Lakes group and has plenty of room for camping as its basin is fairly spacious. Wood is scarce, however, and would have to be carried from the trees about a third of a mile away. Take a backpacking stove and make sure your tent and clothing are adequate for high altitude camping.

NO. 58 – LA GARITA STOCK DRIVEWAY – (West Ute Creek)

Trailhead elevation   –   10,880'
Total vertical ascent   –   2,262'
Highest point   –   12,702'
Total vertical descent –   1,422'
Length –   7.1 miles one way
Maps –   7½' Rio Grande Pyramid
             7½' Storm King Peak
             Rio Grande National Forest
             Rio Grande National Forest Trail No. 787

The section of the La Garita Driveway with which this guidebook is concerned is a 7.1-mile segment that ascends West Ute Creek, crosses Ute Pass and meets the Continental Divide Trail 1.0 mile north of Hunchback Pass. The first 5.0 miles of the driveway apparently have not been used by sheep for some years now. It is likely that the 3.1 miles of the La Garita Driveway in West Ute Creek are most commonly thought of (or referred to) as West Ute

Creek Trail.

The trail begins at mile 6.8 of Ute Creek Trail (No. 54) just after Black Lake. Ute Creek Trail descends to the confluence of the Ute Creeks through the large meadow but the La Garita Driveway keeps right and loses only about 160' of elevation as it heads for West Ute Creek. The trail is not clear at first, probably because everyone takes a slightly different course through the rolling meadows. The U.S.G.S. 7½' quadrangle shows a steep climb into the timber at mile 1.0. You can satisfactorily continue through the meadow although there are a few boggy places but nothing serious. Shortly, there is a very fine view of the Rio Grande Pyramid (13,821') and the Window (La Ventana). The trail becomes very clear as the valley levels out and broadens. It is hard to hurry through beautiful West Ute Creek with its meadowed valley floor contrasting with the steep walls covered with dark timber. The unnamed 13,230' summit just east of Mount Nebo is framed at the head of the valley.

At mile 3.1 West Ute Lake Trail (No. 57) continues up the valley and the La Garita Stock Driveway is somewhat hard to follow as it works its way into the trees to begin the steep climb to Ute Pass. Look for blazed trees and yellow driveway markers about 4" x 5" nailed on trees and by mile 3.5, after crossing a stream the trail is very clear once more. The stream is recrossed and a small meadow is reached. The trail enters the trees again at mile 4.0 and begins the excruciating climb on a 20% grade to Ute Pass (12,702') at mile 5.0.

Once at Ute Pass, which is between a 13,308' summit to the west and a 13,342' summit to the east, the view down into Starvation Gulch is often enhanced by the presence of a large herd of elk which have a summer range there. Descending from Ute Pass, the trail has initially very poor footing in sand as it begins traversing over to Indian Ridge. After walking across the wide meadow on Indian Ridge the trail again loses elevation rapidly as it comes back to timberline (mile 6.25) and soon reaches the jeep road and Bear Creek at mile 6.75.

The drainage of Bear Creek was excluded from the Wilderness because of mineral prospects, and it leaves an unusual 4.0-mile long by 2.0-mile wide indentation in the Wilderness boundary.* Ascending now along the jeep road, the trail climbs past some ramshackle mining cabins and meets the Continental Divide Trail (No. 59) in about 300 yards at mile 7.1.

*Read <u>Stampede to Timberline</u> by Muriel Sibell Wolle for more background on mining in the Bear Creek area and the western end of the Weminuche Wilderness.

VII.
The Continental
Divide Trail

"I look over my shoulder for one last view of the gorge. Like looking down at the bottom of the ocean. People spend their entire lives at those lower altitudes without any awareness that this high country exists."

— From Zen and the Art of Motorcycle Maintenance
Robert M. Pirsig

FIRST PART — to Nebo Pass — mile 11.5
SECOND PART — to Weminuche Pass — mile 28.0
THIRD PART — to Squaw Pass — mile 40.25
FOURTH PART — to Piedra Pass — mile 61.0
FIFTH PART — to Wolf Creek Pass — mile 80.0

The 80.0 mile Continental Divide Trail if taken as a whole may be the most exciting trail in the Weminuche Wilderness. Since 32 of the 59 trails in the guidebook ascend to the Continental Divide Trail it is often used by hikers to connect two ascending trails. Walking the entire Divide Trail from Stony Pass to Wolf Creek Pass (maximum length in the Weminuche) takes the backpacker through the most remote and beautiful sections of the Wilderness. With a few exceptions, the Divide hiker will only encounter others occasionally.

The three lowest places on the Divide Trail are Weminuche Pass (10,622'), Squaw Pass (11,200'), and Piedra Pass (11,400' ; see note on Piedra Pass name in Trail No. 37), and are about the only places where the Divide reaches down to timberline. The average elevation along the Continental Divide Trail is 12,000' + over the 80.0 miles. Because of these facts the Divide Trail requires good stamina and proper equipment if one hopes for a pleasant experience. If available, statistics would be surprising on the numbers of people who began the Divide Trail with the intent of walking it in its entirety and had to abort prematurely. The physical strength needed is primarily in the legs and wind. Constant walking at elevations around 12,000' can produce some lethargy and disorientation even in persons in good condition. In addition, since food and equipment for 8 to 10 days is the maximum that most people will consider carrying, a good deal of walking must be done every day to achieve the objective. One must also try to take into account lost time because of rough weather that is common along the Divide Trail's route. Of course, with food caches located along the trail, weeks could be spent (and deservedly so) enjoying the country enroute. It is not necessary to be a Colin Fletcher but some sort of physical and mental preparations should be made prior to the trip.

Since a good deal of the camping will be at timberline and above, and you are constantly exposed to some of the most varied weather imaginable, your equipment must be first class. Packs that are uncomfortable will be an atrocity by the conclusion of the trip. Tents that are broken or blown away by wind and storm may thrust you into a survival situation. Light-weight but warm clothes and rain-gear are essential. In writing the trail description it is assumed that potential Divide walkers have their equipment problems worked out, so that the main considerations in choosing campsites will be scenery and availability of water.

Almost all the difficulties in route-finding are in the Stony Pass to Weminuche Pass section. From Weminuche Pass to Wolf Creek Pass the Continental Divide Trail follows a single ridge or line of peaks and is clearly defined. In 1975 a new group of 7½' topographic maps became available replacing a 1905, 1/125,000 edition that was the only topographic map for the section from east of Weminuche Pass to Piedra Pass. The new Rio Grande and San Juan National Forest maps now show the Divide Trail with continuity. The Forest Service wages a losing battle with the forces of nature placing signs along the Divide Trail. The lack of coordination between the Forest Service districts responsible for the various sections sometimes makes for a confusing array of names and numbers. No. 813 is given to the Continental Divide Trail by the Rio Grande National Forest; it is called No. 564 in the western end and No. 1564 in the eastern end of the San Juan National Forest. It is also called the Skyline Trail in a section west of Piedra Pass.

The trail description begins at Stony Pass (trailhead B) and ends at Wolf Creek Pass (trailhead S). Since the Divide Trail is easily walked from east to west as well, the western end was chosen for the beginning because of the availability of public transportation to the Silverton area. Stony Pass is approachable on foot or with a 4-wheel drive vehicle (see Trail No. 1). Trail No. 1 or No. 3 and No. 4 are alternate ways of reaching the Divide Trail near its beginning at the western end. The Narrow Gauge Railroad stops at Trail No. 4 and bus service is available to Silverton. Jeeps from a tour agency in Silverton could be hired to transport persons to Stony Pass.

The eastern end at Wolf Creek Pass is easily reached by passenger cars from Highway 160. A 1.7-mile road (Forest Service No. 402) takes you from the summit of Wolf Creek Pass to Lobo Overlook (trailhead S).

FIRST PART — to Nebo Pass — mile 11.5

Total vertical ascent   —   3,133'
Highest point   —   12,840'
(mile 6.75)
Total vertical descent —   3,333'
Maps — 7½' Howardsville
             7½' Storm King Peak
             San Juan National Forest
             Rio Grande National Forest

Beginning at Stony Pass (12,588') under the shadow of Canby Mountain (13,478'), a place of considerable significance for the San Juan Mountains (see note on Trail No. 1), the jeep road has been improved a little in recent years although the western side, toward Silverton, is very steep and rocky. The headwaters of the Rio Grande slope away in alpine tundra and, according to people who saw it in the 1870's and 1880's, 150—300 pack animals could be seen grazing on the eastern side.

The trail begins about 400 yards east of the summit and leaves the jeep road passing an old cabin. The next 3.0 miles have been grazed by sheep for years and there are many strong trails that may bewilder you. The guidebook's map shows a route somewhat closer to the Continental Divide than what is depicted on the U.S.G.S. 7½' quadrangle, which seems a better alternative.

At mile 2.2 Cunningham Gulch Trail (No. 1) is met, and you should keep left of a 150′ grassy summit and skirt a marshy area to continue.

The Divide Trail climbs to a high and wide plateau (about 12,600′ high and 1.0 mile wide on the average) that runs from the vicinity of Highland Mary Lakes to the head of Elk Creek (see detail in Geological Summary). The views southwest into the Grenadier Range are very good. As the trail approaches Elk Creek Trail (No. 4), mile 6.4, a few jeep tracks can be seen although the access from Bear Creek is now closed. Past Elk Creek at mile 6.75 you can look right at Lake Eldorado (12,504′), with White Dome (13,627′) standing behind it. Although a cross-country route that follows the Continental Divide over Hunchback Mountain is developing, the real trail turns left suddenly to descend to Kite Lake (12,100′), mile 7.5. Eldorado or Kite Lakes make good camping places; Eldorado Lake is prettier but Kite Lake is on the way. Kite Lake has an old cabin, a couple of mine shafts and related equipment, and you can almost sense the presence of the mining fever of years ago in this place.

Walking down from Kite Lake on a jeep road, you will see the trail going right after a couple of switchbacks at mile 7.9 and beginning the ascent to Hunchback Pass. It may not show up clearly until you have gone a little ways. From Hunckback Pass (12,493′) at the headwaters of Vallecito Creek at mile 8.8, Hunchback Mountain (13,136′), .75 mile west, could be climbed for a good view. The trail descends a straight, barren valley to meet Vallecito Creek Trail (No. 10) at mile 10.1. From this point, over Nebo Pass to West Ute Lake, the Divide Trail is not shown on the U.S.G.S. 7½′ quadrangle. Here the Divide Trail turns left ascending Nebo Creek and reaching Nebo Pass (12,440′) at mile 11.5.*

At Nebo Pass there is an attractive lake with a tremendous chunk of rock in it. Mount Nebo (13,205′) rears up in spectacular

---

*In mid-August of 1874, Franklin Rhoda who was in charge of a group of men doing the work of the Hayden Survey, crossed Hunchback Pass, climbed Mt. Nebo and had a splendid view of the Grenadier Range and the Needle Mountains. A small grizzly bear was scared up near the summit and disturbed Rhoda's solitude (which must have been well-nigh perfect); and he followed this incident with a diatribe on the degradation of this pristine area. All such judgments are relative; one wonders what Rhoda would think of the 1970's.

cliffs just beyond. An interesting but exposed campsite would be possible here. The view from Nebo Pass west into the Grenadiers is, from left to right: Mount Silex (13,628'), Peak 9 (13,402'), Peak 8 (13,228'), Storm King Peak (13,752') and the sharp Trinity Peaks (13,745', 13,805', and 13,765'). To the east over the Ute Creek drainage, from the left you see Ute Pass (12,702') and purplish-appearing Ute Ridge (13,000' +), Simpson Mountain (12,904'), Rio Grande Pyramid (13,821') and the Window (La Ventana).

SECOND PART — to Weminuche Pass — mile 28.0

Total vertical ascent   —   2,334'
Highest point   —   12,617'
(mile 23.0)
Total vertical descent —   4,075'
Maps — 7½' Rio Grande Pyramid
       7½' Weminuche Pass
       San Juan National Forest
       Rio Grande National Forest

In this section the trail is unclear in several places principally because it is not confined to traversing ridges or winding around peaks. From Nebo Pass the Divide Trail begins descending into a nondescript brushy basin and .25 mile east of Nebo Pass a short cross-country walk north will take you to Clark Lake (12,326'). Continuing downhill with a 13,230' unnamed summit on the right, the trail enters the timber and contours around to meet West Ute Lake Trail (No. 57) at mile 13.2, about 100 yards below West Ute Lake (11,801'). There is plenty of space for camping at the lake as well as in the basin about .5 mile above.

Climbing a 400' ridge the trail then descends a few switch-backs at mile 14.5 and encounters a problem at mile 15.0. At this point a clear trail is seen to descend the little valley before you (this trail reaches Ute Creek Trail in 1.5 miles). You must go south to Middle Ute Lake over a faint or non-existent trail, pass around to the south and begin ascending. The country is covered with mountain willows and you work your way through them toward the eastern end of a smooth-faced, long ridge that lies to the south. By the time you reach the sliderock at the base of the ridge the

Weminuche Pass

trail should become clear once again. Past the ridge at mile 17.0, the trail is on a low divide between the Flint Lakes country to the south and Twin Lakes to the north. A trail descends south to meet Rock Creek Trail (No. 11) in .8 mile. The Divide Trail continues on and descends to Twin Lakes (11,792') and meets the Ute Creek Trail (No. 54), a little to the northwest of the smaller Twin Lake. Here you turn right and walk along the right side of a wide mead-owed valley passing the wreckage of a Colorado Game and Fish Department Super Cub that went down in 1960. At about mile 19.0 the trail passes a small shallow lake, reaches a low ridge and begins descending. After passing Ute Lake (11,847'; about .25 mile north of the trail) Rock Creek Trail (No. 11) is met at mile 19.6. (Flint Lake and Flint Creek Trail No. 17 are 2.0 miles away). From this point the trail climbs to Gunsight Pass (12,360') at mile 20.4. Gunsight Pass is a break in the light-colored crumbling sandstone that encircles half of the basin of Rincon La Osa. De-scending a little ways from Gunsight Pass the trail can be seen climbing up a steep bench while the La Osa Trail (No. 22) drops off to the right. There isn't much trail now as you walk along a 300-yard wide brushy bench to reach East Ute Creek Trail (No. 55) at mile 22.0. The trail is suddenly good from the head of East Ute Creek. Proceed by climbing steeply to a saddle (12,617') at mile 23.0 a little ways north of a black, bristling 13,017' summit. As the trail begins to descend into Rincon La Vaca (Spanish: valley of the cow) through slopes covered with golden-colored alpine sunflowers, Weminuche Pass may be seen far down the canyon as a small patch of green meadow. The Window, 143' high, and the Rio Grande Pyramid (13,821') soon come into view. They have both been important landmarks to travelers in the region since the days of the Spanish gold-seekers and figure prominently in the legends and tales of lost treasure.* People who spend much time in viewing distance of the Pyramid and the Window know that fierce storms seem to linger here, and possibly for this reason, old Mexican

---

*Spanish were supposed to have had a mine in this vicinity in the 1750's. Also, a Captain Stewart found a rich placer in 1852. Troubles with the Utes caused him to leave the region hastily and upon returning, he could not locate the placer again. Read Sheepherder's Gold by Temple Cornelius and Golden Treasures of the San Juans by John Marshall and Temple Cor-nelius, both published by Sage Books.

sheepherders called the Window the "Devil's Gateway."

At mile 23.75, about 200 yards south of a little lake, the trail is easy to lose. Continuing downhill on a brushy ridge and making good use of a topographic map, you will descend further into Rincon La Vaca and eventually to a clear trail. Taking a trail past the little lake and beyond, you can stay close to or on a ridge extending east from the Pyramid and ending at Weminuche Pass in 5.0 miles. This is not shown on the U.S.G.S. 7½' quadrangle. The trail into La Vaca Creek plunges steeply through a narrow canyon and after leveling off somewhat, continues on, reaching some gentle meadows at mile 26.5. Finally, after walking along the left side of Raber Lohr Ditch (read notes about Weminuche Pass in Trail No. 14) the trail crosses the ditch at mile 28.0 and reaches the wide-open Weminuche Pass (10,622').

THIRD PART — to Squaw Pass — mile 40.25

Total vertical ascent   —   3,138'
Highest point   —   12,760'
(mile 35.75)
Total vertical descent —   2,520'
Maps —   7½' Weminuche Pass
             7½' Little Squaw Creek
             7½' Granite Lake
             7½' Cimarrona Peak
             San Juan National Forest
             Rio Grande National Forest

From the crossing of the Raber Lohr ditch at Weminuche Pass, the trail goes south for .3 mile and then turns east. Here you walk straight across the .5 mile of extended meadow to find the Divide Trail at the edge of the timber. In some years Weminuche Pass is very wet and soggy. After entering the timber the trail climbs around a ridge into the dark North Fork of the Pine River and ascends very steeply. The meadow along the North Fork widens and the grade lessens until the stream is crossed. The trail begins to climb again after entering the timber. At mile 31.75 the top is reached. Here, where Snowslide Canyon Trail begins (No. 21; not shown on the U.S.G.S. 7½' quadrangle), the U.S.G.S. map seems to be in error on the Divide Trail. The Divide Trail is shown turning southwest for .5 mile, then south between two small lakes. This is a marshy and brushy route, not recommended. The guidebook's map shows a route south from the Divide between the North Fork and Snowslide drainages, following a couple of postmarkers and passing just east of the cluster of shallow lakes. Once you begin climbing the ridge ahead, the trail becomes very clear. The trail climbs moderately but steadily to where the Continental Divide is a 12,000' sprawling ridge. You have the feeling that you are on top of the world, with vistas all around: to the west, the Needle Mountains, the Rio Grande Pyramid and the Window; to the northeast, the La Garita Mountains which are north of Creede.

When the trail begins to descend to the pass at the head of Grouse Rincon, watch carefully for a large herd of elk who have a summer range in the vicinity. Climbing again the trail meets Squaw Lake Trail (No. 52) at mile 35.25 and a little further on, it switchbacks up to the high point of this section, 12,760'. To the east, in one of the glacial cirques that fall away to Squaw Creek, lies cobalt-blue Squaw Lake. As you begin to descend you can see the rugged volcanic mountains ahead and perhaps even get a glimpse of Navajo Reservoir, approximately 50 air miles south at the border of New Mexico.

The trail descends gently along a ridge through brightly colored flowers, such as paintbrush and moss campion, for about .5 mile. It then switchbacks and drops steeply to pass through a series of cirques deeply gouged into the impressive and unnamed volcanic summits that average around 13,000'. To the east, Chief Mountain (13,014') looks massive. Numerous small lakes are scattered throughout the three basins and, to my knowledge, have not all been tested for fishing. Around these lakes are any number of beautiful campsites. The Forest Service maps are completely wrong through this section indicating a line of travel over the peaks on the Divide. However, the new U.S.G.S. 7½' quadrangle accurately depicts the trail here. Climbing a rough ridge at mile 38.0 to reach the next basin, the trail descends, crosses Squaw Creek close to its source and enters the timber. Snow may linger in the trees and obscure the trail up to the end of July. The meadows of Squaw Pass (11,200') are reached at mile 40.25. Hossick Creek Trail (No. 25) goes south from Squaw Pass at this point.

FOURTH PART — to Piedra Pass — mile 61.0

Total vertical ascent   —   5,232'
Highest point   —   12,400'
(mile 42.5)
Total vertical descent —   4,722'
Maps — 7½' Cimarrona Peak
        7½' Little Squaw Creek
        7½' Palomino Mountain
        San Juan National Forest
        Rio Grande National Forest

From the top of Squaw Pass, meadows extend down Squaw
Creek for as far as you can see to the north and into a fork of
Williams Creek for about .75 mile to the southwest before a steep
drop-off. A little past Hossick Creek Trail junction, Squaw Creek
Trail (No. 51) goes left to descend the well-glaciated Squaw Creek.
The Divide Trail soon enters the trees and begins to climb around
to a small canyon where a few switchbacks assist in gaining elevation. The Forest Service maps incorrectly show the Continental
Divide Trail to the east and in Williams Creek drainage for a few
miles after Squaw Pass. The high point of this section (12,400')
is reached at mile 42.5, about 1.0 mile south of the summit of
Chief Mountain. Now winding along a line of peaks, the Continental Divide Trail meets Williams Creek Trail (No. 28) at mile 43.5,
and views down into the headwaters of Little Squaw Creek show a
drainage very similar to Squaw Creek's but without a trail. At mile
44.5 the Divide Trail makes a long jog southeast to ascend a ridge
of a 12,740' unnamed summit above Trout and Williams Creek
Lakes.

Descending 350' the trail crosses the divide between the lakes
and meets Williams Lake Trail (No. 29), and .5 mile south of Trout
Lake, meets Trout Creek Trail (No. 47). The Divide Trail continues
around the left (north) side of a 12,430' summit and approaches
the Knife Edge. Along the steep north face leading up to the Knife
Edge, the remains of the previous winter's snowslides can last into
mid-summer. If you are the first person on this part of the Divide
Trail, it will take some time to stomp out a decent set of tracks.
The precipitous volcanic cliffs of the Knife Edge fall away sharply
below the trail. Once around the jagged and tortured Knife Edge,

On the Continental Divide Trail near Wolf Creek Pass

which juts out about 1,000' above the surrounding countryside, the trail descends to a basin. Cherokee Lake (11,600') is reached at mile 47.75, with its 800' warbonnet above the lake to the north.

Past Cherokee Lake the Divide Trail climbs and begins traversing a group of high, whale-backed ridges. The footing is like walking in sand as you slog through the gravelly porphyry that makes up these ridges which fall away quickly on either side producing an airy feeling. At mile 49.7 the Palisade Meadows Cut-off (No. 31) leaves the ridge and the Continental Divide turns east. After about one mile, the Divide goes somewhat lower and the average elevation will be closer to 11,700' for the next 10.0 miles with frequent stretches of timber. Water is scarce in this part unless you go down off the Divide. At mile 53.0 the saddle is reached where the Indian Creek Cut-off (No. 32) descends and at the saddle just south of a 12,000' baldy-type mountain, Indian Creek Trail (No. 30) is located. There are no signs for No. 30, No. 31 or No. 32.

Now the Divide Trail turns east to contour around four basins at the head of East Trout Creek which is good country for sighting elk. To watch a large elk herd grazing, with the calves frolicking around the adults, gives one a supreme feeling that all things are right and tranquil insofar as the wilderness is concerned. At mile 56.5 Middle Fork Trail (No. 33) goes to the right (south) of a golden-hued summit (12,310') and the Divide Trail continues to a sort of pass where East Trout Creek Trail (No. 48) is met. Views to the east reveal the ellipsoid 12,328' Piedra Peak and behind it, 13,149' South River Peak. Past some white, gaping gullies of porphyry the Divide Trail goes through a basin below 12,230' Palomino Mountain and turns east to begin the descent to Piedra Pass. At mile 59.0 the trail passes left of a 12,067' summit and through a rough section of red and copper-colored sliderock to enter the timber. Before reaching Piedra Pass (11,400') at mile 61.0, you will have to crawl over some fallen timber.

FIFTH PART — to Wolf Creek Pass — mile 80.0

Total vertical ascent —   4,520'
Highest point   —   12,880'
(mile 63.0)
Total vertical descent —   4,480'
Maps — 15' Spar City
       15' Wolf Creek Pass
       San Juan National Forest
       Rio Grande National Forest

At Piedra Pass, Turkey Creek Trail (No. 37) goes south just after entering the meadows but the Continental Divide Trail continues along a diversion ditch for a few hundred yards until another ditch with a measurement gate is seen. East of that, the Divide Trail ascends through the timber by a small sign saying: Continental Divide Trail No. 1564. The West Fork Trail (No. 38) goes south (right) along the second diversion ditch.

The Divide Trail passes through a stretch of downed trees and soon reaches an open grassy basin below South River Peak. Watch for the post-markers to guide you as the trail climbs steeply to the highest point of this section (12,880') at mile 63.0. South River Peak (13,149') is only .25 mile away along Fisher Creek Trail (No. 46) and views from here on a clear day include the Sangre de Cristo Range to the east and, beyond the major portion of the Wilderness, the La Plata Range to the west. The trail rounds two summits of nearly 13,000' and begins a switchbacked descent with a look into the wild-appearing Beaver Creek Canyon. The next 9.0 mile of the Divide to Archuleta Lake are the most exposed and open of the entire trail and water is hard to find without leaving the Divide, so fill a water container at any opportunity. The Continental Divide through this section is a series of humps and ridges which the trail is constantly climbing or descending. At mile 68.0 Sawtooth Trail (No. 45) is reached. In about 1.0 mile the hard-to-see Beaver Creek Trail (No. 39) is met. Where the Divide Trail peeks into Hope Creek's basin at mile 69.75, it meets the Highline Trail (No. 43) which has climbed around 12,605' Sawtooth Mountain .75 mile north of this point.

The Continental Divide Trail continues on and climbs a ridge of whitish Mount Hope (12,834') and begins the steep descent to

Archuleta Lake (11,680') at mile 72.0. Archuleta Lake Trail (No. 40) can be found in the trees at the east end of the lake. In .75 mile the Divide Trail passes Spotted Lake and climbs a steep ridge extending east from a 12,304' unnamed summit on the Divide. The trail descends to and contours around a forested basin and after passing Spruce Reservoirs (unseen), it reaches meadows at the head of the South Fork of the Rio Grande. At mile 75.5 South Fork Trail (No. 41) goes left and the Divide Trail climbs through a sliderock slope abundant with marmots and pikas. The trail passes a spruce-bounded lakelet at mile 76.5, which frames distant Mount Hope very nicely. The vista down the South Fork canyon is of a dense, dark forest that covers acres and acres uninterrupted. As the trail proceeds along the ridge it passes through several meadows filled with lush green grass and many high-altitude flowers such as cutleaf daisies, elephant's head, and paintbrush. The Continental Divide Trail reaches the Lobo Overlook (trailhead S) at the edge of the Weminuche Wilderness at mile 80.0.

SUGGESTED READING LIST

Geology: Physiographic and Quaternary Geology of the San Juan Mountains, Atwood and Mather; Geological Survey Professional Paper 166, 1932.

Rocks and Minerals, Zim and Shaffer; Golden Press, 1957.
Good introduction

New Mexico Geological Society Guidebook of the Southwest San Juan Mountains, New Mexico Bureau of Mines and Mineral Resources, 1957.

Prairie, Peak and Plateau, John and Halk Cronic; Colorado Geological Survey Bulletin No. 32, 1972.
Acquaints reader with general Colorado geology

Red Rock Country, Donald Baars; Doubleday Natural History Press, 1972
Good sections on the San Juans

Landforms, Adams and Wyckoff; Golden Press, 1971.

History: (sections of these books are pertinent)

The Great Gates, Marshall Sprague; Little & Brown Co., 1964.
Passes on the Continental Divide

The Great Surveys of the American West, Richard Bartlett; University of Oklahoma Press, 1962.
Contains good information of the Hayden Survey

Stampede to Timberline, Muriel Sibell Wolle; Sage Books, 1969

Golden Treasures of the San Juans, Marshall and Cornelius; Sage Books, 1961.

Sheepherder's Gold, Temple Cornelius; Sage Books, 1964.

Flora and   Trees of North America, Frank Brockman; Golden
Fauna: Press, 1968.

              Field Guide to Rocky Mountain Wildflowers, John and
              Frank Craighead and Ray Davis; Houghton Mifflin Co.,
              1963.

              Field Guide to Western Birds, Roger Tory Peterson;
              Houghton Mifflin Co., 1961.

              Field Guide to Mammals, Burt and Grossenheider;
              Houghton Mifflin Co., 1964.

              Field Guide to Animal Tracks, Olaus J. Murie; Hough-
              ton Mifflin Co., 1954.

              Rocky Mountain Treefinder, Tom Watts; Nature Study
              Guide, 1972.
                        Good introduction to trees of the area; small
                        for carrying in pack.

Back-   Backpacking One Step at a Time, Harvey Manning;
packing: Vintage Books, 1973.

              The New Complete Walker, Colin Fletcher; Alfred
              Knopf, 1975.

              Instructive Catalogs: REI Catalog
                                      P.O. Box 22090
                                      Seattle, Wa. 98122

                                      Eastern Mountain Sports Catalog
                                      Box 924
                                      Boston, Ma. 02215

Medical: Being Your Own Wilderness Doctor, Kodet and Angier;
              Pocket Books, 1972.

              Survivit, Dr. Loren Johnson; Survivit, 1973.
                        Compact and lightweight for backpacking.
                        To order: Survivit
                                    Lake McQueeney, Texas 78123

Mountains: The Fourteeners, Eberhart and Schmuck; Sage Books,
              1970.

              Guide to the Colorado Mountains, Robert Ormes; Sage
              Books, 1970.
                        A climbing guide.

APPENDIX

Services for backpackers in communities adjacent to the Wilderness

CREEDE

San Juan Hiking Service and Supply
P.O. Box 81
Creede, Colorado 81130
(303) 658-2359

Backpacking equipment, sales and rental, clothing, freeze-dried food, topographic maps

DEL NORTE

Mac's Sporting Goods
660 Grand
Del Norte, Colorado 81132

Topographic maps

DURANGO

Alpine Sports
707 Main
Durango, Colorado 81301
(303) 247-1935

Backpacking equipment sales and rental, climbing equipment clothing, freeze-dried food, topographic maps

Four Faces Outdoor Sports
144 West Tenth Street
Durango, Colorado 81301
(303) 247-0500

Tents, sleeping bags, clothing, maps and supplies

Gardenswartz
863 Main Avenue
Durango, Colorado 81301
(303) 247-2660

Backpacking equipment sales, climbing equipment,
clothing, freeze-dried food, topographic maps

The Outdoorsman
949 Main Avenue
Durango, Colorado 81301
(303) 247-4066

Backpacking equipment sales, clothing, freeze-dried
food, topographic maps

Pine Needle Mountaineering
Main Mall
835 Main Avenue
Durango, Colorado 81301
(303) 247-8728

Backpacking equipment sales, climbing equipment,
clothing, freeze-dried food, topographic maps

PAGOSA SPRINGS
Pagosa Ski Rentals
Pagosa Springs, Colorado 81147
(303) 264-2866

Backpacking equipment sales, climbing equipment,
clothing, freeze-dried food, topographic maps

SILVERTON
Timberline Trading Company
Silverton, Colorado 81433

Backpacking equipment sales, climbing gear, clothes,
freeze-dried food, topographic maps

SOUTH FORK

Brown's Country Store
South Fork, Colorado 81154
(303) 873-5582

Topographic maps

Moon Valley Lodge
Box 265
South Fork, Colorado 81154

Equipment rental

U.S.G.S. 1:24,000 quadrangles along with free indices for each
state can be ordered for $1.25 each from:

U.S. Geological Survey
Branch of Distribution
Central Region
Box 25286, Federal Center
Denver, Colorado 80225

Upon request, they will include a helpful pamphlet explaining
topo maps.

San Juan National Forest Supervisors Office
Federal Building
P.O. Box 341
Durango, Colorado 81301
(303) 247-4874

>   responsible for trails:
>   No. 1—No. 8. . . . . .Animas Ranger District
>   Federal Building
>   P.O. Box 761
>   Durango, Colorado 81301
>   (303) 247-5912
>
>   No. 9—No. 22. . . . . . . .Pine River District
>   Bayfield, Colorado 81122
>   (303) 884-2512
>
>   No. 23—No. 34 . . . . . . .Piedra Ranger District
>   P.O. Box 368
>   Pagosa Springs, Colorado 81147
>   (303) 968-2268
>
>   No. 35—No. 39 . . . . . . .Pagosa Ranger District
>   P.O. Box 368
>   Pagosa Springs, Colorado 81147

Rio Grande National Forest Supervisors Office
1803 West Highway 160
Monte Vista, Colorado 81144
(303) 852-5944

>   responsible for trails:
>   No. 40—No. 43 . . . . . . .Del Norte Ranger District
>   810 Grand Avenue
>   Del Norte, Colorado 81132
>   (303) 652-3321
>
>   No. 44—No. 58 . . . . . . .Creede Ranger District
>   Creede, Colorado 81130
>   (303) 658-2425

DENVER and. . . . . .Tickets and information about
RIO GRANDE WESTERN   Narrow Gauge Railroad
479 Main
Durango, Colorado 81301
(303) 247-2733

TRAIL NOTES